"*The Mystic Way of Evangelism* is about evangelism, which is truly important obviously for our mainline churches that are aging and declining but no less for our evangelical churches that are far less effective in evangelism than they often think. But Elaine Heath's book is about much more than evangelism. It's about a richer, deeper approach to Christian faith. It offers a fresh perspective on church history, and it addresses the relevance of the gospel to contemporary problems. Here's my hunch: for many readers, this will be the most important book they read this year."

—**Brian McLaren** (brianmclaren.net), author/activist

"Elaine Heath has produced a remarkably creative work, linking the church's missional priority for evangelism with the neglected resources of the church's mystics. To do this, she confronts contemporary issues in ministry by opening a treasure trove of theological insight and mystical practices, including both current innovations and past centuries of Christian devotion. Within these pages are both a vigorous challenge to the church and a way for robust spiritual renewal of the faith to flourish."

—**William B. Lawrence**, dean and professor of American church history, Perkins School of Theology, Southern Methodist University

"Elaine Heath provides a narrative by which to understand what is happening within the mainline church, as well as throughout Christendom, through her use of the classic threefold contemplative path from night through illumination to union. Her use of this path provides both insight and hope for those who seek to be faithful to Christ and the church. Other books on evangelism have not always resonated with the 'mystic' within us, nor have they emphasized the importance of justice in evangelism. Heath's challenge to engage in eco-evangelism is essential in regaining the church's moral authority in the present global climate crisis."

—**Sally Dyck**, resident bishop of Minnesota, The United Methodist Church

The MYSTIC WAY of EVANGELISM

A CONTEMPLATIVE VISION FOR CHRISTIAN OUTREACH

Elaine A. Heath

Baker Academic
a division of Baker Publishing Group
Grand Rapids, Michigan

Published by Baker Academic
a division of Baker Publishing Group
P.O. Box 6287, Grand Rapids, MI 49516-6287
www.bakeracademic.com

Printed in the United States of America

Library of Congress Cataloging-in-Publication Data
Heath, Elaine A., 1954–
    The mystic way of evangelism : a contemplative vision for Christian outreach / Elaine A. Heath.
        p.   cm.
    Includes bibliographical references and index.
    ISBN 978-0-8010-3325-4 (pbk.)
    1. Evangelistic work. 2. Witness bearing (Christianity). 3. Missions. 4. Mysticism. I. Title.
BV3770.H38 2008
269′.2—dc22   2008017345

Scripture quotations are from the New Revised Standard Version of the Bible, copyright © 1989, by the Division of Christian Education of the National Council of the Churches of Christ in the United States of America. Used by permission. All rights reserved.

For my mother, Helen Louise Madon Heath

Contents

Acknowledgments

In so many ways this book reflects the wisdom and love of those who have joined me in my journey. I especially want to thank my dear friends, the late Betty Jeavons, Morven and David Baker, Jerry Flora, Mary Ellen Drushal, and John Jorden. Mind-sharpening, soul-enriching conversations with colleagues have been invaluable, especially those with William Thompson-Uberuaga and William J. Abraham. I am so grateful to work with diverse and incredibly gifted colleagues at Perkins School of Theology. Much of the work that I have done in this book began in discussions with my students, who ask wonderful, difficult questions and who teach me far more than I teach them. Along those lines I especially appreciate the probing questions of former students JoAnn Shade and Nick Swirski, as well as current students at Perkins School of Theology and my graduate assistants Mark Teasdale and Ken Loyer. Many thanks are also due to my editors at Baker Academic. I am indebted more than I can express to faithful intercessors who prayed for me as I wrote.

My deepest gratitude goes to my beloved husband, Randall Bell, a true contemplative who exemplifies and inspires in many of us a life of faith, hope, and love.

Introduction

My first foray into the world of evangelism took place when I was six years old. My family did not attend church. My parents were, in fact, hostile to Christianity, having been exposed too many times to a form of Christian witness that was shaming, exclusive, bigoted, and in other ways unsavory. Despite their aversion to all things relating to church, they did allow us children to attend church if we wanted to go with a neighbor or friend, because it got us out of the house on Sunday mornings, providing them an oasis of peace and quiet. Thus I found myself at the age of six in Sunday school for the first time, sipping Kool-Aid, coloring a picture of Zaccheus the Wee Little Man, and listening to the teacher talk about a place called hell. Upon my return my mother asked how I liked Sunday school. I told her I liked the snack and the story but was worried about hell. It sounded like a pretty bad place. The teacher had said that everyone who smokes and drinks is going to hell, which was bad news for Mom and Dad.

That was the end of my Sunday school career for a while, and the introduction to my parents' hermeneutic of suspicion toward the church. It was also the beginning of a lifetime of questioning the meaning of evangelism: a pursuit that not only shaped my journey with my family, all of whom eventually became faithful disciples of Jesus (in some cases in spite of my early efforts to evangelize them), but also my vocation as pastor and teacher. Ultimately the quest led me to write this book.

Many volumes have already been written to explore the history of Christian missions, the biblical mandate for advancing the reign of God, the best techniques with which to share one's faith, and practical suggestions for congregations to become more evangelistic. These are all of value and I have used many of them in research and teaching. Yet there is a striking absence in most contemporary discussions of evangelism of the wisdom of the great spiritual giants—the Christian mystics—to shape and lead our understanding of the theory and practice of evangelism. I find this absence particularly significant in light of a postmodern hunger for mysticism of all kinds, and in light of the remarkably shallow to nonexistent practice of evangelism in so many contemporary American churches. The church is in trouble in the post-Christendom West, the kind of trouble that requires leadership from those who are holy. The great Christian mystics are our exemplars of holiness. In their lives and written texts we find what has been lacking but is needed in our theory and practice of evangelism.

Defining Evangelism for the Church

The loss of the robust, holistic primacy of evangelism in the theology and practice of the church is reflected in comments my students make at the start of every semester. My students are, by the way, wondrously diverse. On the first day of class I ask students to name three things they want to learn about evangelism. At least half the students respond that they wonder if it is possible to share their faith without "shoving it down people's throats." Some students want to know if evangelism has anything to do with social justice, or if it is even a Christian activity in light of the history of the Inquisition, Crusades, colonialism, and American "manifest destiny." In a globalized, religiously pluralistic world, some students ask, is evangelism exclusive, fundamentalist, destructive? Doesn't it contribute to international hostility and religious violence? Their comments reflect a general mistrust and misunderstanding of evangelism in the church, and expose some of the wounds that Christians have inflicted on the world in the name of evangelism. Their questions also reveal the inadequacy of programmatic approaches to evangelism in the local church.

Happily, many of the skeptical students undergo a kind of conversion during the semester, as they come to understand that real evangelism is never coercive, violent, or exploitive. Real evangelism is not colonialism, nationalism, or imperialism. Evangelism rightly understood is the holistic initiation of people into the reign of God as revealed in Jesus Christ.[1] The process of evangelization is expressed in three categories of activities introduced to the church by Jesus: preaching, teaching, and healing.[2] Evangelism includes all aspects of the initiation of persons into the holy life, including catechesis, individual and corporate spiritual disciplines, participation in the sacraments (or ordinances, in some communions), and active membership in the life and mission of a local faith community. Evangelism as an initiatory process is complete only when individuals are fully incorporated into the church, participating in the life of the church in worship, service, prayer, and evangelistic presence in the world. This means that evangelism really is at the heart of everything we believe and practice as Christians. As Watchman Nee might have said were he involved in the conversation today, evangelism is at the core of the "normal" Christian life.[3]

Evangelism is intrinsically relational, the outcome of love of neighbor, for to love our neighbor is to share the love of God holistically. The proper context for evangelism is authentic Christian community, where the expression of loving community is the greatest apologetic for the gospel. Holiness—being given to God and God's mission in this world—is a way of life that is expressly concerned with evangelism. To be holy is to be set aside exclusively for God's purposes, to be the 'olah or whole offering that is a living sacrifice, according to

---

1. I am indebted to William J. Abraham for his definition of evangelism as initiation into the kingdom of God (*The Logic of Evangelism* [Grand Rapids: Eerdmans, 1989], 95). Scott Jones builds on Abraham's definition in *The Evangelistic Love of God and Neighbor* (Nashville: Abingdon, 2003), 112–18.

2. Matt. 9:35–38.

3. Watchman Nee (1903–1972) was a leader of the Chinese house church movement who spent the last twenty years of his life in prison for his faith. His most famous book is *The Normal Christian Life* (1957; repr., Wheaton: Tyndale, 1977).

Paul in Romans 12:1–2.[4] We are not set aside and made holy for our
own pursuits; we are now in partnership with God in God's mission.
Paul explains in Romans 8 that we are now "heirs and joint-heirs
with Jesus," the liberator whose mission is to redeem all of creation.
The holiness of God's people provides both hope and agency in the
transformation of the world.

For this reason, the great exemplars of holiness—the Christian
mystics—are without exception the first and best teachers of the
theory and practice of evangelism. Their contemplative vision of the
love of God and the redemptive purposes of God in the world shatter
our programmatic and market-driven assumptions about evangelism.
Their passionate surrender to Christ exposes imperialistic, exploitive,
and manipulative versions of evangelism, and highlights the falsity
of accusations that evangelism is just one more way the church is in
collusion with the world. Spiritual giants such as Julian of Norwich,
John Woolman, and Mechthild of Magdeburg speak with an authority
the church desperately needs today. These mystics are the incarnation
of faith, hope, and love, the holy ones who can illumine the dark path
on which the Western church finds itself.

About Christian Mysticism

To further my proposal that the mystics are the best teachers of evangelism, a brief identification of Christian mysticism is in order. For
readers from traditions in which mysticism is not an ordinary category
of theological inquiry, clarification may be needed to define and dis-
tinguish Christian mysticism from other kinds of mysticism.

Some Christians resist all talk of mysticism, as if mysticism and
Christianity were mutually exclusive. The great Methodist mystic[5]

4. More will be said throughout this book as to what constitutes holiness, with the
great saints and mystics as exemplars of holy people. For now, the important points
are that holiness is about being given over completely to God out of love for God,
and about how holiness expresses itself in love of neighbor.

5. Palmer's mysticism was the source of her altar theology and the fountainhead
for her powerful evangelistic ministry. Palmer is said to have led as many as twenty-
five thousand people to "saving faith in Christ," in a ministry that in every way was
equal to that of Charles Finney (Ruth Tucker and Walter Liefeld, *Daughters of the*

and mother of the holiness movement, Phoebe Palmer, was herself opposed to what she called "mysticism" because of her narrow understanding of the term.[6] Yet as Anne Taves demonstrates, Christian mysticism has always been present in the Methodist tradition.[7] Indeed, the mystical element of religion is necessary for the Christian religion to remain truly Christian, according to Friedrich von Hügel, whose landmark work *The Mystical Element of Religion* opened the way for new explorations of Christian mysticism in the academy.[8]

Mysticism, contrary to popular belief, is not essentially about private numinous experiences. The earliest Christian use of the word *mustikos* was in relationship to God's revelation in Christ, of that which was previously hidden.[9] Christian mysticism is grounded in the revelation of Jesus Christ. Colossians 1:26–27 is an example of this understanding. As time passed, the meaning of Christian mysticism evolved to include Christ revealed in the incarnation, in the Eucharist, in Scripture, and in the community of faith.

Christian mysticism is about the holy transformation of the mystic by God, so that the mystic becomes instrumental in the holy transformation of God's people. This transformation always results in missional action in the world. The idea that mysticism is private and removed from the rugged world of ministry is simply false. All the Old Testament prophets were mystics. Their visions, dreams, and other experiences of God were for the express purpose of calling God's people back to their missional vocation.

Those who could properly be called the great Christian mystics, such as St. John of the Cross, attained a radical degree of holy transformation as a result of their encounters with the Triune God.[10]

Church: Women and Ministry from the New Testament Times to the Present [Grand Rapids: Academie, 1987], 263).

6. Phoebe Palmer, *Full Salvation: Its Doctrine and Duties* (Salem, OH: Schmul Publishing Co., n.d.), 146–47.

7. Ann Taves, *Fits, Trances and Visions: Experiencing Religion and Explaining Experience from Wesley to James* (Princeton, NJ: Princeton University Press, 1999).

8. Friedrich von Hügel, *The Mystical Element of Religion* (1923; repr., New York: Crossroad, 1999), 50–84.

9. Mark A. McIntosh, *Mystical Theology* (Malden, MA: Blackwell, 1998), 24.

10. William M. Thompson, *Christology and Spirituality* (New York: Crossroad, 1991), 5.

That is, their inward transformation resulted in an outward life of extraordinary impact on the world. All the great Christian mystics were prophets with a vision for God's mission in the world. Most of them suffered the rejections and persecutions prophets encounter from stiff-necked religious folk.

Ecstatic Experience

But what about mysticism and ecstatic experiences? The word "ecstasy" comes from the Greek word *ekstasis*, which means to go out from (*ek*) a standing or "static" position (*stasis*). Authentic Christian ecstatic experiences are God-initiated movements of the Holy Spirit that lead Christians beyond themselves to greater identification with God and God's mission in the world. Genuine ecstatic experiences always propel the Christian (and the church) into mission.

Christian mysticism is grounded in the church, the Body of Christ.[11] It is the God-initiated experience of being moved beyond oneself into greater depths of divine love. This movement results in an inward transformation of wholeness and integration and an outward life of holiness, an increasing love of God and neighbor. Mysticism has epistemological significance in that the experience of God is a participatory knowing. The divine encounter of mysticism carries profound authority for those who experience it, a fact overwhelmingly present in the call experiences of many of the great reformers and in the stamina of the mystics as they endured persecution at the hands of the church.

Apophatic and Kataphatic

Two terms should be defined to help navigate the conversation throughout the book. These terms are "apophatic" and "kataphatic" and are usually used as adjectives to describe mysticism, spirituality, or theology (e.g., the apophatic theology of Meister Eckhart or the kataphatic spirituality of St. Ignatius).

11. Ibid., 9.

Apophatic mysticism refers to the *via negativa* or what is sometimes called the way of "unknowing," for although God is revealed to us in nature, the Bible, and especially in Jesus, our comprehension is limited by our finitude. We "see through a glass darkly." We tend to fixate on specific aspects of God's self-revelation as if they were exhaustive, particularly God as Father and *only* as Father, when God is actually much more than Father and the many other images God has given us. We can know God through God's self-revelation, but we cannot know God exhaustively. Because our Triune God is uncreated, God cannot be known or described as just one more "thing," in the way we might describe a plant or a human or the earth. God is no "thing."[12] Apophasia is in part the process of growing in our understanding and experience of God, who is more than we can ever exhaustively know and whose depths are to us a divine and beautiful mystery. This part of apophasia has to do with not knowing, with mystery.

By extension apophatic mysticism also includes aspects of negation or self-emptying (*kenosis*) in the spiritual journey: the renunciation of one's own agenda, the purification of ego and all that is involved in "dying to self." Spiritual advancement in the apophatic way involves, among other things, a detachment from an idolatrous clinging to religious images, forms, rituals, human traditions, and experiences, so that their place in the spiritual life can be cleansed and realigned.

At times discussion about apophatic mysticism can itself become a bewildering "cloud of unknowing" because of the negative language many of the old mystics use about nothingness, dark nights of the soul, detachment, emptiness, letting go, not knowing, and so forth. Yet genuine apophatic mysticism is not so much about personal, subjective, inner experiences of "darkness" and nothingness as it is about a *de-emphasis* or relativization of experience.[13] Part one of this book is particularly concerned with purgation, the cleansing aspect of apophatic mysticism, in relation to the church in the United States.[14]

---

12. Christian apophatic mysticism can help to "protect" Christian spirituality from panentheism, in a spiritually syncretistic world.

13. McIntosh, *Mystical Theology*, 23. This insightful distinction is of particular importance in chapter 4, in regard to the apophatic mysticism of Phoebe Palmer and Father Arseny.

14. Contemporary discussions around apophatic mysticism hail this form of spirituality as the one most helpful in building bridges of understanding between

One of the primary themes of this book is the life of kenosis, or self-emptying, which is a key expression of the apophatic way.

In contrast to and in creative tension with apophatic mysticism is kataphatic mysticism, which is, conversely, a path of spiritual advancement in which images, forms, subjective spiritual experiences, creation, incarnation, and discursive thought all lead to union with God. Kataphatic mysticism is the most notable form of mysticism found in the Hebrew prophets. It is a mysticism of affirmation (*via affirmativa*), with God as the source of all that exists.[15] God speaks to Moses in a burning bush, not in silence and nothingness. The prophet Ezekiel sees visions of God, as do Isaiah, Jeremiah, Amos, and others. In the New Testament the incarnation of Jesus adds to the Old Testament foundation of the kataphatic way. As the Apostle Paul writes, "[Christ] is the image of the invisible God, the firstborn of all creation . . . for in him all the fullness of God was pleased to dwell" (Col. 1:15, 19). Stories of mystical visions, dreams, actions, experiences, and encounters can be found throughout the New Testament. Indeed, kataphatic mysticism is overwhelmingly present in the New Testament. Thus it is safe to say that from a standpoint of Scripture alone, Christian mysticism must include the kataphatic. Again, however, it is important to note that Christian mysticism is not essentially about kataphatic experience or the apophatic de-emphasis on experience; it is essentially about the transformation of God's people.

Mysticism, Evelyn Underhill writes, "is essentially a movement of the heart, seeking to transcend the limitations of the individual standpoint and to surrender itself to ultimate Reality; for no personal gain, . . . purely from an instinct of love."[16] Mystics are irresistibly

---

Christian and non-Christian spiritual traditions, since some form of apophatic spirituality is present in all major religious traditions of the world. From a standpoint of evangelism, knowledge of a broad spectrum of apophatic traditions is enormously helpful for faith-sharing in a religiously pluralistic world. See John Sahadat, "The Interreligious Study of Mysticism and a Sense of Universality," *Journal of Ecumenical Studies* (Spring 1985): 294–96; William Johnston, *Arise My Love: Mysticism for a New Era* (Maryknoll, NY: Orbis, 2000); and Harvey D. Egan, "Christian Apophatic and Kataphatic Mysticisms," *Theological Studies* 39 (September 1978): 399.

15. Johnston, *Arise My Love*, 116–17.

16. Evelyn Underhill, *Mysticism* (New York: Meridian, 1955), 71.

drawn to become one with God and God's purposes in the world. Underhill dryly comments that the true mystic is the one who "attains to this union, not the person who talks about it."[17]

The mystic, then, is one for whom the immediate presence of God and the drawing of God toward union are lived, fundamental realities. God's presence is both immanent and transcendent, transforming the mystic inwardly while compelling him or her to an outward life of increasing love and compassion.[18] The radical transformation of mysticism is a possibility for any believer and is really what God has in mind for all Christians.[19] Yet the reality is that many Christians do not appear to attain, in this life at least, radical transformation. Thus while mysticism or mystical experiences may be found among believers who are at different levels of spiritual maturity, the one who could properly be called a mystic seems to be much less common.

Regardless of the presence or absence of specific mystical experiences—including visions, dreams, prophetic foreknowledge, spiritual combat, dark nights of the soul, and other phenomena—for all mystics there is a process of growth into increasing holiness.[20] Whether the mystic is predominantly apophatic or kataphatic in his or her experience, the result of Christian mysticism is an ever-increasing capacity to love God. The greatest "proof" of mysticism is its fruit: love of God and *neighbor*. This is a love that is enfleshed in action. Mysticism brings about prophetic action that is compassionate and sacrificial, the Eucharistic life in which God's people become "broken bread and poured out wine"[21] for the world. The Eucharistic life is always evangelistic.

---

17. Ibid., 72. Bernard McGinn prefers the term "presence" rather than "union," finding it more useful in describing the "immediate or direct presence of God" in and through the mystics (Bernard McGinn, *The Presence of God*, vol. 1, *The Foundations of Mysticism* [New York: Crossroad, 1992], xv–xvii).

18. Underhill, *Mysticism*, 90.

19. Thus the title of another of Underhill's books, *Practical Mysticism* (Columbus, OH: Ariel, 1986).

20. Underhill, *Mysticism*, 75–90.

21. This is a favorite phrase of Oswald Chambers in describing the Eucharistic life. See Oswald Chambers, *My Utmost for His Highest* (New York: Dodd, Mead & Co., 1935), 33, 41, 46, 56, 136, 197, 274, 320.

The Threefold Way

The following chapters are organized into three parts named after the classical threefold contemplative path: purgation, illumination, and union. In part one, purgation is presented as a process the church must go through to be revitalized and to reclaim its prophetic, healing, evangelistic presence in the world. Chapter 1 describes the decline of the church in the United States using the conceptual framework of the threefold contemplative path, advancing the proposal that the decline is best understood as a corporate dark night of the soul. Because this is a process that the church must go through, it means that the night is initiated by God and could lead the church to a new and vibrant life.

Part two, "Illumination," presents the key elements of a contemplative vision for evangelism that should characterize the church emerging from the night. Each chapter is thematic, drawing from the life and writing of two mystics, demonstrating the centrality of the theme of how we should *think about* evangelism. These themes include: love as God's meaning, holiness for the sake of the world, coming home to God's love, healing, and the redemption of creation. The first of these themes, love as God's meaning, should be understood as primary, integrating the other four themes into a unified whole. The church in the night will be able to emerge from its torpor only as it is cleansed and healed of its brokenness in these five areas.

Julian of Norwich called union with God the "one-ing" of the soul. Part three, "Union," casts a vision for ways in which the church can take a contemplative stance, evangelistically living in union with God in day-to-day life. Each of the chapters in part three include a narrative portraying one possible model for a contemplative church that reflects the embodiment of the themes presented in part two. I have chosen narrative theology for this part of the work because it makes the most sense to postmodern readers and because it is evocative rather than attempting to be exhaustive in describing the contemplative church. Narrative theology serves the contemplative way better than many other forms of theology.

In keeping with this theme, a portion of each of the final chapters includes the unfolding story of a man named Sam and his process of evangelization in a church that embodies a contemplative stance. The story is simple and plain, in keeping with the contemplative way, yet has enough descriptive elements to demonstrate the life-giving difference a contemplative stance could make. This story presents just one possible form of church in order to inspire creativity, prayer, and change. It is not meant to be the only form of church that will "work," and thus slavishly imitated. While I have seen various elements of this church in different real congregations and communities, the composite of First Church belongs just to this story. The people in Sam's story are not meant to represent individuals known to me. Any similarities to actual people or situations are coincidental.

It is my prayer that this volume furthers theological conversation about evangelism, drawing from the wisdom of the mystics to hear afresh the meaning of the good news, as well as the spirit in which we are to share it. Because this is a book offering an intentionally contemplative vision for evangelism, the genre is spiritual theology, integrating analysis with narrative theology in an invitation to a holy life. As Tyler Roberts notes, approaching the topic in this "space between" devotional account and analysis opens the possibility of creative new questions, not only about the religious topic at hand but also about the way we study all aspects of religion.[22] This book is not intended to be exhaustive but is an introduction to a contemplative vision for evangelism. My deepest hope for this book is that it will contribute in some way to the formation of evangelistic leaders and congregations who will be able to reach postmoderns with the news that is, indeed, very good.

22. Tyler Roberts, "Between the Lines: Exceeding Historicism in the Study of Religion," *Journal of the American Academy of Religion* 74, no. 3 (September 2006): 699.

PART ONE

PURGATION

1

Into the Night

A dark night of the soul is descending on the church in the United States. The signs are everywhere: a steady decline in church membership, especially among mainline denominations;[1] a striking increase in the percentage of Americans who do not attend church;[2] dropping numbers of young adults preparing for ordained ministry;[3] the loss of moral authority and credibility among clergy and churches due

1. For statistical data on decreasing membership among three of the largest mainline denominations see "Methodists See More No-Growth Churches," *Christian Century* 123, no. 8 (April 18, 2006): 16; "Presbyterian Losses Largest Since '83," *Christian Century* 121, no. 13 (June 29, 2004): 13; and "Data Bite," *Christian Century* 120, no. 18 (September 6, 2003): 13. For National Council of Churches 2001 statistics on church membership in nine of the largest denominations in the United States see "Benevolences Up, Membership Stable: 2001 Yearbook Reports," www.ncccusa.org/news/01news15 .html. While statistical data suggests continued growth among conservative evangelical denominations such as the Southern Baptists and Assemblies of God, the percentage of growth among evangelical churches does not account for all the losses in mainline denominations. In other words, a significant number of members leaving mainline churches leave the church altogether.

2. Between 1991 and 2004 there has been a 92 percent increase in unchurched people, according to the Barna Group ("Number of Unchurched Adults Has Nearly Doubled since 1991," *The Barna Update,* May 4, 2004, www.barna.org/FlexPage .aspx?Page=BarnaUpdate&BarnaUpdateID=163).

3. Andrew C. Thompson, "Decline in Young Leadership Threatens Methodism's Future," *United Methodist Reporter* 152, no. 52 (May 5, 2006): 7B. For some of the reasons young adults eschew ministry as a vocation see David J. Wood, "The Con-

to widespread sex scandals and financial misconduct at the hands of clergy;[4] an increasing hermeneutic of suspicion toward the church by the Internal Revenue Service; and other forms of distancing between American civic and religious life.[5] With the growth of religious pluralism and spiritual syncretism in postmodern culture, the church's historic primacy as America's spiritual and moral compass continues to erode. As Philip Jenkins notes, while the church (especially Pentecostalism) is growing rapidly in the southern and eastern hemispheres, the era of Christendom in the United States is over.[6]

Many Christians view the decline of Western Christendom with alarm, as if God had fallen from heaven. Enormous effort is put forth to launch church growth programs to shore up membership, increase giving, and keep denominational ships afloat. But the history of God's people is a history of life cycles, a history of clarity about call and identity, followed by complacence, followed by collusion with the powers, followed by catastrophic loss. Contrary to being a disaster, the exilic experiences of loss and marginalization are what are needed to restore the church to its evangelistic place. On the margins of society the church will once again find its God-given voice to speak to the dominant culture in subversive ways, resisting the powers and principalities, standing against the seduction of the status quo. The church will once again become a prophetic, evangelistic, alternative community, offering to the world a model of life that is radically "other," life-giving, loving, healing, liberating. This kind of community is not possible for the church of Christendom. Christendom

ditions of Call," *Congregations* (March–April 2001), www.alban.org/ShowArticle .asp?ID=114.

4. Ted Olsen and Todd Hertz, "How the Clergy Sexual Abuse Scandal Affects Evangelical Churches," *Christianity Today* 46 (March 20, 2002), www.christianity today.com/ct/2002/110/31.0.html.

5. After a guest preacher, George F. Regas, delivered an antiwar, antipoverty sermon on October 31, 2004, at All Saints Episcopal Church in Pasadena, California, church officials were notified that the church would be audited by the IRS, specifically because of the sermon's political statements. The sermon was delivered two days before the presidential election. For details on this and other recent events in which Christian organizations have come under governmental scrutiny for their positions on social justice, see OMB Watch, "IRS Audits Church for Anti-War Sermon," www.ombwatch .org/article/articleview/3167/1/403.

6. Philip Jenkins, *The Next Christendom* (New York: Oxford University Press, 2002), 3.

opposes prophetic community with its upside-down power and its exposure of golden calves.

Thus Walter Brueggemann describes the declining Western church as the church in exile, comparing it to the Jews exiled in Babylon. The church's exile is cultural rather than geographic, but holds the same kind of disorientation, anxiety, and intensity of grief over the glory having left the temple.[7] Brueggemann disturbs us with the reminder, "In the end, it is God and not the Babylonians who terminated the Temple project."[8] Ironically, to once again become evangelistic in the healthiest, most holistic sense, the church in America needs the "severe mercy" of great loss.

The dark night of the soul is precisely that—a divinely initiated process of loss—so that the accretions of the world, the flesh, and the devil may be recognized and released. It is a process of detachment from disordered affections, a process of purgation and de-selfing.[9] Though the dark night is perilous, with no guarantee of a good outcome, it holds the possibility of new beginnings. Out of the night the church could emerge into a dawn of freedom and fidelity.

The dark night is here, even now. While the sun sets on Christendom in the West, the saints, mystics, and martyrs beckon to the church as a great cloud of witnesses, calling us to transformation. The church will persevere through the night and emerge alive on the other side, not because of church programs, but because God's love has kept it.[10] But to get there, we need the wisdom of the mystics, the holy ones of God.

The Gift of Detachment

While many Christian mystics and saints have described experiences of a dark night, the term is associated primarily with John of the

7. Walter Brueggemann, *Cadences of Home: Preaching among Exiles* (Louisville: Westminster John Knox, 1997), 1–3, 11–12. Darrell Guder, Lois Barrett, et al., see the loss of missional ecclesiology as the core issue behind declining Christendom (Darrell Guder, ed., *Missional Church* [Grand Rapids: Eerdmans, 1998]).

8. Brueggemann, *Cadences of Home*, 109.

9. Underhill, *Mysticism*, 397.

10. Julian of Norwich, *Showings*, Classics of Western Spirituality, ed. Edmund College and James Walsh (New York: Paulist Press, 1978), 183.

Cross, the sixteenth-century Spanish Carmelite whose stunning poem *Dark Night of the Soul* continues to challenge and nourish Christians from many spiritual traditions. The depth and breadth of meaning in John's ascetical theology is beyond the limits of this discussion and has been well-described from diverse perspectives.[11] John distinguishes between active and passive nights of the senses, and active and passive nights of the spirit, for example. Each of these aspects of the night is purgative, freeing the soul from attachments that hinder the ability to receive and give God's love. Jessie Penn-Lewis, writing more than three hundred years later from the Keswick movement, described the dark night using her own language and pneumatological framework, which, though less intricate than that of the great Carmelite reformer, contains the same general meaning. The night is the time to surrender the "spiritually religious self," religious views, old ways, thought patterns, and activities that have become idolatrous substitutes for God in and of themselves. "If we surrender even the manifest presence of God, we become rooted and fixed in God. Not that He wants to take all away, but He wants us to surrender, that He might reveal himself as an abiding reality."[12] In consideration of the process of the night for the church, then, it is helpful to take a broader view of the night as described from a wider theological spectrum rather than a narrow, strictly Carmelite perspective.

In the Bible we find many stories of God's people in the night. Sometimes in these narratives the night has to do with the apparent thwarting of the divine call or promise in an individual's life. We see this in Joseph's years of imprisonment in Egypt, Moses's decades as a shepherd, David's long years of exile during Saul's increasingly

11. For an introduction to the writings and a variety of contemporary reflections on John of the Cross see John of the Cross, *Selected Writings*, Classics of Western Spirituality, ed. Kieran Kavanaugh and Ernest E. Larkin (New York: Paulist Press, 1987); Susan Muto, *John of the Cross for Today: The Dark Night* (Notre Dame, IN: Ave Maria Press, 1994); Hein Blommestijn et al., *The Footprints of Love: John of the Cross as Guide in the Wilderness*, trans. John Vriend (Louvain: Peeters, 2000); Francis Kelly Nemeck and Marie Theresa Coombs, *O Blessed Night* (New York: Alba House, 1991); and Gerald May, *The Dark Night of the Soul: A Psychiatrist Explores the Connection between Darkness and Spiritual Growth* (San Francisco: HarperSanFrancisco, 2004).

12. Jessie Penn-Lewis, *Fruitful Living* (Dorset, UK: Overcomer Literature Trust, n.d.), 19–20.

paranoid reign. The night is also revealed in God's people as they experience the seeming absence of God during times of oppression or suffering. It is revealed in the barren yearning of Sarah, Leah, and Hannah, in Habakkuk's complaint, in Jeremiah's anguished cry, and in the mystery of Job's suffering. The dark night reaches its climax in the cry of Jesus on the cross: "My God, my God, why have you forsaken me?"[13]

The detachment described by so many who have traversed the night is often from religious rigidity, or from religious activity that has become in itself a god. This detachment takes place gradually, sometimes imperceptibly, at other times with great struggle and grief. Often those who are in the night are unaware of the nature of their attachments, especially religious attachments. One thinks of Nicodemus, for example, who surreptitiously questioned Jesus about the spiritual path. Nicodemus was unable to name for himself the religious ossification that prevented him from seeing the kingdom of God, though there were intimations drawing him to Christ.[14]

Gerald May notes, "Sometimes this letting go of old ways is painful, occasionally even devastating. But this is not why the night is called 'dark.' The darkness of the night implies nothing sinister, only that the liberation takes place in hidden ways, beneath our knowledge and understanding."[15] One of the clear signs of a dark night is its very obscurity, as if an opaque veil protects the cleansing, purifying work.

The cumulative effect of the dark night when embraced by God's people is the deconstruction of self-centeredness and the removal of subtle idolatry in terms of mistaking God for religious feeling and activity, or created things, or viewing God as one more "thing." God is *nada*, no "thing." The dark night brings about a necessary detachment so that God's people may freely love all things in and through the love of God rather than in and of themselves. Religious activities, rituals, and practices especially are cleansed so that they are now, in the oft-quoted imagery of Thomas Merton, fingers pointing to the

13. Hans Urs von Balthasar (see chapter 2) sees Jesus's solidarity with humanity in such complete terms that the cry of Jesus on the cross, his experience of godforsakenness, and his descent into hell are all to be taken literally and seriously.

14. John 3:1–21.

15. May, *The Dark Night of the Soul*, 5.

moon and no longer mistaken for the moon itself. The fruit of the night is about the transformation of relationships into expressions of love of God and neighbor, and love of self for the sake of God.[16]

May is correct in his assessment that John of the Cross has often been misunderstood by subsequent interpreters, especially when used to promote negative images of God.[17] For the love of God is present and active in the night, bringing about growth, healing, and freedom, gifts of detachment from enmeshed relationships, compulsions, addictions, and idolatries that are not immediately apparent to those who have yet to emerge from the night.[18]

In some sense the emergence from the night is never complete in this life, for the process of God's leading to further growth and freedom in obscurity is lifelong. It is part of the process of sanctification, of being made holy. The three parts of the contemplative path—purgation, illumination, and union—are simultaneous rather than sequential, but our human finitude prevents us from seeing their simultaneity, so that we perceive of them as being distinct phases. Even so, the night may still be described in a cyclical sense, for the purgation of the night waxes and wanes, along with seasons of illumination and moments of union.

Language about detachment requires careful interpretation, especially when reading texts arising from apophatic spirituality. Rather than being a process of complete separation from people and things we love (though at times it does mean separation), detachment in this context is best understood as the transformation of one's relationships with self, others, the created world, and God, so that increasingly one "holds loosely" all loves, with open hands and heart. To hold loosely is to let go of fearful clutching and control, and is to set

---

16. Here the insights of Bernard of Clairvaux (1090–1153) in his teaching on the "four degrees of love" are helpful. These are progressive, with the fourth and ultimate degree occurring only intermittently in this mortal life. The four degrees are: love of self for self's sake, love of God for self's sake, love of God for God's sake, and, finally, love of self for God's sake (Bernard of Clairvaux, "Four Degrees of Love," in *Invitation to Christian Spirituality*, ed. John R. Tyson [New York: Oxford University Press, 1999], 149–53).

17. Ibid., 8.

18. For a thorough discussion of the value of John's theology for those in recovery from addictions, see Nemeck and Coombs, *O Blessed Night*.

free that which is loved.[19] This kind of liberating love grows slowly, gradually, and is not possible aside from the work of the night, for we are burdened with many attachments, addictions, and idolatry. We all struggle with "disordered affections," to use the language of Ignatius of Loyola.[20]

With this brief introduction to the conceptual framework of the first part of the threefold contemplative path, purgation, let us turn our attention to the American church of the early twenty-first century. Let us think about the church in terms of the signs of an impending night, which are (1) dryness and fruitlessness in prayer, religious activity, and life; (2) a loss of desire for the old ways of being religious; and (3) a growing desire simply to be with God.[21]

Dryness and Fruitlessness

The decline of mainline churches in America has been under way for decades, with a staggering loss of membership, the closing of churches, and a graying and dwindling of the flock. The widespread failure to evangelize younger generations is reflected in the rising age of clergy. In the United Methodist Church, for example, during the last twenty years the number of ordained elders under the age of thirty-five has plummeted from 3,219 to 850.[22] Once the largest and most robust Christian movement in North America, the United Methodist Church (UMC) has recorded annual losses in membership and church attendance for decades (more than 70,000 members in 2004, for example). Having enjoyed a membership of more than 8 million since the 1930s, in 2008 UMC membership is expected to

19. Sting captures the spirituality of this kind of liberating love, and the perennial problem of clutching and controlling those we love, in his song "If You Love Somebody, Set Them Free," *The Very Best of Sting and the Police*, A&M, 2002.

20. The Ignatian spiritual exercises are a systematic method of prayer and self-examination to help identify disordered affections and progress in the spiritual life. See Ignatius of Loyola, *Spiritual Exercises and Selected Works*, Classics of Western Spirituality, ed. George E. Ganss (Mahwah, NJ: Paulist Press, 1991), 113–214.

21. These are nicely summarized in contemporary language in May, *Dark Night of the Soul*, 138–41.

22. Lovett H. Weems Jr., "Leadership for Reaching Emerging Generations," *Circuit Rider* (March–April 2006): 4–7.

drop below 7,989,875, with worship attendance at its "lowest level in reported history."[23] Similar patterns are found in the Presbyterian Church (USA), with a projected loss of 85,000 this year.[24] These kinds of losses or failure to grow are reported in virtually every mainline denomination in America.[25]

Evangelicals like to think that with the growth of megachurches, such as Saddleback and Willow Creek, and the vibrant growth of evangelical and Pentecostal Christianity in the rest of the world, the decline of the church in America is limited to the mainline. Statistics say otherwise. During 2005 the number of baptisms in the Southern Baptist Church, the largest denomination in America, declined 4.15 percent, following a trend that started several years ago with only a modest rebound in 2004.[26] According to the National Council of Churches' 2006 *Yearbook of American and Canadian Churches*, of the twenty-five largest denominations or communions of churches, only four reported an increase of membership.[27] The remaining twenty-one denominations reported either no change or a decrease in membership.

23. Linda Green, "United Methodist Attendance Rises, But Membership Continues Down," www.umc.org/site/c.gjJTJbMUIuE/b.880375/k.EA3C/United_Methodist_at tendance_rises_but_membership_continues_down.htm; General Council on Finance and Administration, The United Methodist Church, "2005 Preliminary Statistics Report Executive Summary," www.gcfa.org/2005PreliminaryStatisticsReportExec Summary.pdf.

24. John H. Adams, "Big Losses Predicted in the PCUSA," *The Layman Online*, www.layman.org/layman/news/2006-news/big-losses-projected.htm.

25. There are some exceptions, such as the .89 percent increase in the Catholic Church and the 6.40 percent increase of the Orthodox Church in America in 2004, yet immigration rather than evangelism may be the primary reason for these increases. See National Council of Churches, "2006 Yearbook of Churches Reflects Robust Immigrant History in US," *News from the National Council of Churches*, www .ncccusa.org/news/060330yearbook1.html.

26. The Christian Post, "Southern Baptists Decline in Baptisms, Make Evangelism a First Priority," *The Christian Post* (April 20, 2006), www.christianpost.com/ article/church/2605/section/southern.baptists.decline.in.baptisms.make.evangelism .first.priority/1.htm.

27. Ibid. Finke and Stark explain the growth and decline of American churches using the tools of marketing analysis, concluding that churches decline when they become secularized and theologically liberal, losing their evangelical fire (Roger Finke and Rodney Stark, *The Churching of America 1776–2005* [New Brunswick, NJ: Rutgers University Press, 2005], 8, 11, 246).

Membership statistics are only one symptom of the increasing aridity of the American church. The loss of giving is another. Robert Wuthnow describes the growing crisis of financial problems in the church. Because churches of all sizes are riddled with financial problems, many small congregations are closing, while larger historic congregations struggle to stay afloat in massive, expensive church buildings from an earlier era. Even newer congregations are struggling financially with debt and utility costs for large buildings erected too quickly in the rush to establish a new church.[28]

Beset with the rising cost of health insurance for clergy and staff, facility maintenance, and other financial pressures, many congregations feel unable to survive, much less to thrive as missional outposts in the world. Increasing numbers of small churches cannot afford a full-time pastor and are opting instead for part-time, bivocational clergy, many of whom lack sufficient theological education.

While these numeric signs of increasing "dryness and fruitlessness" are significant, there are other, deeper indicators of a loss of vitality in the American church. The accommodation of the church to the consumerism, competitiveness, and individualism of postmodern culture is pervasive, from the opulent lifestyle of prosperity gospel preachers to the ubiquitous "worship wars" to pseudoevangelistic "transfer growth" as churches cater to Christians who shop around for a better deal. The fruitlessness is experienced by renewal-minded pastors who are appointed to dysfunctional congregations, where they experience abuse and contempt; by evangelistic and prophetic lay people who are stifled by insecure clergy; by pathological church board members who think that because they are "big givers" they own the church and the pastor; by a frenetic grab for every new church-growth program and strategy that comes along because denominations, judicatories, congregations, and pastors know that if the trend continues their church will not survive; by broken women and men who long to find a spiritual community and come home to God, only to be rejected for the unforgivable sin of divorce; by women who are called and gifted by God for pastoral ministry, only to be silenced or

28. Robert Wuthnow, *The Crisis in the Churches* (New York: Oxford University Press, 1997), 3.

driven out because of gender. Aridity and fruitlessness are found in the consumeristic objectification of prayer, as if prayer were something that should be "tried" because it "works."

In the midst of this desert we find ourselves face-to-face with our attachments, with the pantheon of religious idols, large and small, that have supplanted the God we claim to worship.

Loss of Desire

And so, here in the spiritual desert, in the night of increasing aridity, God's people search through all the familiar patterns, activities, choices, and ways, all the old options that used to provide a sense of religious stability, of spiritual meaning. We think about all the ways we worked to get people to join the church and realize that often what we really wanted was enough money in the offering to pay the utility bills. We sift through the labels we have used to define our own and others' religious identity: liberal, conservative, fundamentalist, saved, unchurched, Spirit-filled, carnal, Pentecostal, Bible-believing, middle of the road, orthodox. "Is *this* what it means to be the church?" we ask ourselves.

Redoubling our efforts we buy an old school bus to start a Sunday school bus program but can't find children for the bus; we hold bake sales and chicken dinners to raise money to pay for a new church bell tower but the new tower doesn't attract new people; we hold revivals and have special musical events but only a handful of "faithfuls" come; we chastise people from the pulpit for their busyness and their absence, their unwillingness to tithe, and their children's soccer games on Sundays; we wonder why, when those children graduate from high school, they graduate from church, and we blame the secular world for this failure. Whatever happened to the days when all the Sunday school classes were filled and the parking lot overflowed?

We look around, stunned and grief-stricken at our own impotence. It is as if all the familiar religious furniture was packed into a great moving van and carried to a far country, but none of it fits in the new house, and the old house has been torn down and we are now foreigners living in a world we do not know. After a while we sit down, exhausted from all our efforts, and think about calling it quits. We keep asking ourselves why nothing works anymore. We lose the desire to try.

The unutterable weariness initiates for some people, both clergy and lay, a disillusioned exodus from the church. They simply walk away. Some do leave for greener pastures, hoping the church with the Anglican liturgy, or the church with the praise band, or the church with a better children's program will fill the longing. For others this giving up of what used to be is the beginning of a long bitterness, a grim campaign to remain in the church but resist all things new, all ideas, dreams, and plans for revitalization, all talk of change. For some weary pilgrims hope still flickers, however dimly, calling forth yearning for love and community, for spiritual life. The way to get there is a mystery hidden in the obscurity of loss. What is not obscure at this time, what is perfectly clear to these weary but hopeful pilgrims, is that most of the elements of church that used to seem essential were nothing more than fingers pointing to the moon. What a church needed to be a church and to be evangelistic, it seemed, were the organ, the stained glass windows, the praise choruses, the new carpet, wafers and little cups instead of intinction for communion, the altar rail, the bulletin, the donor plaques fastened to every piece of furniture in the building, the women's missionary society, the handbell choir, the committees, the youth lock-ins, the mother-daughter banquets, the stoles and vestments, and the projector and screen.

They were fingers that somehow became the moon.

This is the second sign of the night: the flailing, the striving, and the eventual loss of desire for what used to bring satisfaction; the relinquishment of the old furniture along with the old house and the old country. In the night, this detachment is bound to the third sign, which is the unremitting longing for the presence of God in the midst of so much loss. The emptying of the night prepares a readiness for the God who is beyond all our systems and forms and institutions, whose presence calls into question everything we thought about church.

A Holy Longing

The reassessment of all that we have known as church, as God-with-us-the-community-of-faith, is precisely where we find ourselves today. Throughout and beyond our denominations Christians are yearning for a simpler, unfettered relationship with God in community, for a new day for the church.

It is a holy longing, this yearning in the night. It leads to the freedom necessary for illumination. And so the church in America is in transition, with Christendom fading into memory and the religious accretions of the world, the flesh, and the devil, increasingly apparent for what they are. We are in a time of chaos and confusion, an ecclesiastical *tohu wabohu*[29] over which the Spirit of God broods and speaks. We are ready for a different way to think about our vocation as the church. It is time for us to discover a contemplative vision for evangelism.[30]

29. *Tohu wabohu* is the richly nuanced phrase of Gen. 1:2, in which the raw material of creation is chaos and confusion, over which the Spirit of God hovers to bring forth ordered life.

30. The image of the Christian life as a living flame is found in many of the mystical texts, including the title of one of John of the Cross's poems (John of the Cross, *Selected Writings*, 285–316).

PART TWO

ILLUMINATION

2

Love Is God's Meaning

Far beyond the confines of Christendom in their times, in breathtaking, world-encompassing visions of redemption, Julian of Norwich and Hans Urs von Balthasar opened windows into the sinful world *as God sees it*. Though living some six centuries apart, in very different worlds, for each of them the compelling reason to share the good news of the gospel was love instead of fear, hope instead of judgment. In postmodern culture with its religious pluralism and syncretism, Julian's and Balthasar's vision is a compelling apologetic for global evangelism. We live in a violent world of abuse, poverty, exploitation, and environmental disasters, a world in which we are both perpetrators and victims of sin. Into this world Julian and Balthasar speak the unfathomable love of God that, they assure us, will have the last word.

In this chapter we will explore the profound insight of Julian into original wounds, and reflect on Balthasar's nonpunitive doctrine of atonement, a perspective shaped in part by Julian's theology. Drawing from their wisdom, we will then consider a different perspective on human brokenness, the universal context for evangelization.

Julian's World

Julian, a fourteenth-century[1] anchorite of Norwich, England, spent
most of her life in a small cell attached to the Church of St. Julian,
from whom she took her name. As an anchorite, her life was devoted
to prayer, not for herself but for the world.[2] She lived during an
era of horrific suffering. Three times during Julian's life, bubonic
plague swept through Europe, the first outbreak decimating as much
as a third of the population of England and half the population
of Norwich. The Hundred Years' War raged, a peasants' revolt in
England was brutally subdued (with support from the church), and
Lollards were marched to their martyrdom just outside Norwich. In
the midst of all this, Julian lived, prayed, and ministered, grounded
in her central conviction that the universe belongs to a God who
is love, that eventually "all manner of thing shall be well." Overwhelmed with grief, anxiety, and incomprehensible loss, countless
people found their way to the curtained window in Julian's cell.
There they found sanity, healing, forgiveness, and peace. They found
Christ. Julian became, in the midst of their shattered world, the
apostle of hope.[3]

Julian's wisdom arose from a lifetime of meditation on a series
of sixteen visions she experienced on May 8, 1373,[4] while gravely ill.
She was just thirty years old at the time, and her mother and several

1. Julian lived from 1342 to about 1416.

2. Anchorites were solitaries who felt a call to the contemplative life, spending their lives in a single room attached to a church. In the manner of the earliest
monastics of Egypt, they were not members of an order but lived their individual
religious vocation directly under God. Although they spent much time in solitude,
they usually had a window through which they offered what we today might call
pastoral counseling and spiritual direction. In Julian's day, the vocation of anchorite
was respected, fulfilling an important role in the church and community. For more
on anchoritic spirituality, see Anne Savage and Nicholas Watson, trans. and eds.,
"*Ancrene Wisse*" *and Associated Works,* Classics of Western Spirituality (New York:
Paulist Press, 1991).

3. For the scant details that are known about Julian's life, see Nicholas Watson
and Jacqueline Jenkins, eds., *The Writings of Julian of Norwich* (University Park, PA:
Pennsylvania State University Press, 2006), 7–10; Robert Llewelyn, *All Shall Be Well*
(New York: Paulist Press, 1982), 2–8; and Julian of Norwich, *Showings,* 17–21.

4. Some manuscripts give the date as May 13, 1373, which is Julian's unofficial feast
day in the Anglican church (Watson and Jenkins, *Writings of Julian,* 4).

other people were with her. The visions began when, after having received last rites, she fixed her gaze upon a crucifix the priest had placed within view. All the visions focused on the passion of Christ and were a complex, visual, mystical theology that included all the major themes of systematic theology, richly informed with Scripture and the tradition of the church. The focus of her theology was redemption—how the Triune God sees human sin and what God does about it. Julian wrote two accounts of the revelations: a short text, apparently close to the time of the visions, and a much longer text some twenty years later. Since the early 1970s several translations of her work and a wealth of material has been written about Julian and her theology, some for popular audiences and much for the academy. Though it is tempting to draw out the many themes of Julian's work that are pertinent to evangelism, our focus in this discussion must be limited to Julian's brilliant insight into sin emerging from original wounds.

During the first fifteen visions, Julian saw to her astonishment that God's judgment is without wrath, that it will heal the entire cosmos. She saw that God looks at human sinfulness and brokenness "with pity and not with blame."[5] Yet how could it be, Julian questioned, in light of sin, the devil, and the traditional teaching of the church, that God's judgment would be without wrath? Julian wrestled with God, unable to resolve the tension between what God showed her and what the church taught:

> The first judgment, which is from God's justice, is from his own great endless love, and that is that fair, sweet judgment which was shown in all the fair revelation in which I saw him assign to us no kind of blame. And though this was sweet and delectable, I could not be fully comforted only by contemplating it, and that was because of the judgment of Holy Church, which I had understood before, and which was continually in my sight. . . . And by the same judgment I understood that sinners sometimes deserve blame and wrath, and I could not see these two in God.[6]

5. Julian of Norwich, *Showings*, 149, 154, 226, 245, 257, 266, 271, 281, 282, 336, 338.
6. Ibid., 257.

Bewildered by the absence of God's wrath (as she understood it) in her visions, as well as God's silence concerning the damned, Julian wept, begging God to give her some way to reconcile the tension. She believed in damnation but could not see it. Knowing the seriousness of sin in the world, she could not grasp how God looked at sin "with pity and not with blame." God's answer to Julian's apophatic dilemma[7] came wordlessly, in the form of the sixteenth and final vision, "the Servant Parable,"[8] which though incomprehensible to her at first became the central narrative in Julian's thought.[9]

As Julian looked "with the eye of her spirit" she saw a handsome lord dressed in luxurious blue clothing. His pale brown face and lovely black eyes bespoke compassion, mirth, mercy, wisdom, and love. Though stately and regal, his presence was welcoming, most "familiar" and "courteous."[10] The lord sat in a vast, empty place, alone except for one servant. The servant wore a thin, shabby tunic, tattered from much hard labor, yet the servant himself was as youthful and fresh as if he had never worked. The servant's sole delight was to serve his lord.

The lord asked the servant to carry out a special task—to till the earth, grow a special food that is hidden in the earth, and bring it back to the lord. Julian marveled that the lord would want anything from the earth since within himself he contained everything, including "all the heavens." The servant, eager to carry out his master's bidding, ran happily to fulfill the task. In his haste the servant fell into a ravine, causing him seven wounds: severe bruising, bodily clumsiness, physical weakness, mental blindness and confusion, the inability to rise again, profound loneliness, and confinement to a narrow, comfortless place. The most astonishing pain to Julian was the servant's sense of utter aloneness in his fallen condition. The servant did not know his lord could see him, did not know the great love that yearned for his recovery.

7. Ibid.

8. The parable (chapter 51) is not found in the short text due to Julian's need to contemplate it for several years before being able to write about it. The implications of the parable, after years of contemplation, greatly enhanced her understanding of all the other "showings," thereby increasing the length of the long text.

9. Julian of Norwich, *Showings*, 269.

10. Julian employs courtly language throughout her work, emphasizing the kenotic love that is expressed in God's dignity and majesty (almightiness), manifesting itself in God's tender, maternal love and God's servanthood.

Deeply moved at the suffering of his beloved servant, the lord was present to every detail. The lord did not blame his servant for the fall because the servant fell from a childlike eagerness to serve his lord. Rejoicing over his servant's love, the lord planned a reward for his servant that surpassed what the servant would have received had the fall never occurred. The lord defends the original intent of the servant who fell:

> See my beloved servant, what harm and injuries he has had and accepted in my service for my love, yes, and for his good will. Is it not reasonable that I should reward him for his fright and his fear, his hurt and his injuries and all his woe?[11]

Julian goes on to say that "the wonder of the example never left me, for it seemed to me that it had been given as an answer to my petition." For the next twenty years "less three months," Julian pondered the meaning of the parable that was "full of secrets," as is the case "with every showing."[12] God told her to pay attention to every detail of the vision, no matter how small, for every aspect of it had revelatory significance. God urged her to contemplate this vision no matter how "mysterious and ambiguous" it seemed, for in due time she would gain insight from it.[13]

As the years passed and Julian prayed, she came to understand that the lord in the parable represents God, who patiently awaits the perfecting of his city. The city is all people who will be saved,[14] for God's intent has always been to dwell within his people, just as his people dwell within him. In a manner reminiscent of the famous drawing that is simultaneously an old woman and young woman,[15] the servant

11. Julian of Norwich, *Showings*, 268–69.

12. Ibid.

13. Ibid., 270. Wai Man Yuen comments that the twenty-year span between Julian's visions and the writing of the long text was actually a dark night of the soul, primarily experienced as ignorance (apophasia) in the face of revelation. Using Augustine's theory of memory, she offers a persuasive argument for the integrity of Julian's authorship of the long text (Wai Man Yuen, *Religious Experience and Interpretation: Memory as the Path to the Knowledge of God in Julian of Norwich's Showings* [New York: Peter Lang, 2003], 1–4).

14. Julian of Norwich, *Showings*, 272.

15. For the famous W. E. Boring figure of the old woman/young woman, with commentary, see Illusion Works, L.L.C., "Perceptual Ambiguity," http://psylux.psych

represents both Adam (corporate humanity) and Christ,[16] humanity's
fall and the incarnation. At one level the servant's fall represents the fall
of humanity, cast not as willful or proud rebellion, but as a consequence
of childlike exuberance leading to a mistake. Most important, the fall
is about wounds: alienation, blindness, fear, suffering, humanity's inability to extricate itself from its fallen place—in short, wounds to body,
mind, and spirit. There are seven wounds, a number that in medieval
religious thought represents completion, thus all the possible wounding
consequences of the fall. At another level the servant's fall represents
Christ "falling into the Virgin's womb" and then into death and hell
in order to redeem humanity.[17] Julian marvels because "in all this our
good Lord showed his own Son and Adam as only one man."[18]

God would no sooner assign blame or wrath to us, Julian argues,
than he would to his own beloved Son, who has taken into himself
for all time the wounds and brokenness of the world. In utter solidarity with all humanity Jesus experienced crucifixion and death, then
descended into hell where he performed a mighty deed: "he raised
up the great root out of the deep depth, which rightly was joined to
him in heaven."[19]

Julian's God loves with a power that is deeper than sin, that heals
all wounds, a love that binds humanity to God forever. Love is God's
meaning, God's essence. God's love is the hermeneutical key for all
theological paradox, all unanswered eschatological questions. God's
overwhelming message to her is one of security for the saved. Even
though she believes in the genuine possibility of hell for people, Julian's stance becomes one of great hope for all people who are the
wounded servant in the ravine.

A "great deed" will take place in the future, a mysterious act that
could never be guessed and that Julian herself does not understand.[20]

.tu-dresden.de/i1/kaw/diverses%20Material/www.illusionworks.com/html/percep
tual_ambiguity.html.

16. In Pauline terminology, first and second Adam (1 Cor. 15:21–22, 47–49).

17. Julian of Norwich, *Showings*, 270–72.

18. Ibid., 275.

19. Ibid., 277.

20. Here again Julian embraces the apophatic reality that she has seen unspeakable
mysteries that she cannot understand or describe, but that have led her into liminal
space (ibid., 240).

This deed will consummate the final healing of the cosmos.[21] Because of this hope it is foolish and counterproductive for Christians to speculate about perdition. Rather, we should contemplate God, whose love is sure and whose redemption will prevail.[22]

Julian draws on Aquinas's vocabulary of "substance"[23] to explain the inseparability of Christ and those who will be saved. There is an inviolable and divine "substance" in the union of Christ with Adam that is found in the deepest will of those who will be saved. Because of the substance there is an aspect of the will that never truly wants to sin. This deepest will against sin may not be conscious to the one who sins, as symbolized by the fallen servant's mental confusion and blindness. Yet by grace the divine substance remains in the will.[24]

The maternal grace of God draws and protects the sinful soul from the moment the soul is breathed into the body, Julian writes.[25] Within our very sensuality (physicality) exists an operation of the Holy Spirit that mysteriously inclines us to God.[26]

Julian's hope for the salvation of all people takes seriously the pervasive reality of sin and its effects.[27] She understands Jesus's suffering as having taken the sin of the world on himself. Julian acknowledges that "our failing is dreadful, our falling is shameful, and our dying is sorrowful." Yet she locates sin in the context of wounds, offering a therapeutic vision of redemption. No matter how dreadful our condition, the "sweet eye of pity is never turned away from us, and the operation of mercy does not cease."[28] How should Christians view sin? First, sin is not a "substance" or a created thing, thus it does not have

21. Julian does see that the devil, whom she calls "the fiend," is already damned, although the final manifestation of his damnation will not be seen until the end of all things (*Showings*, 201–2). Thus her vision of hope does not extend to the salvation of Satan or the demons.

22. Ibid.

23. Aquinas, *Summa theologiae*, 1.8.3.

24. Julian of Norwich, *Showings*, 283.

25. Ibid.; cf. 297–300.

26. Ibid., 287.

27. It is important to keep in mind that Julian does not fully endorse universalism, nor was she ever censored by the church for her eschatology or any other aspect of her theology. Her focus, rather, is radical hope for all people and security for "all who will be saved."

28. Julian of Norwich, *Showings*, 262.

eternal existence and cannot be known except by the pain it causes.[29] Sin is forgivable. Christians should willingly accuse *themselves* of the sins they commit, Julian advises, particularly in light of the pain it costs the Lord. The reason for such self-examination, however, is not to lead to self-loathing or despair, but toward appreciation for Christ's great love for them, and to see their tremendous worth in God's eyes.[30] To God, humanity is worth any suffering that is required to bring about redemption. Thus Christians should view all people as those beloved by God and worthy of redemption, capable of being forgiven and healed of their wounds. All people are worthy of hope.

It was precisely this aspect of Julian's theology—her therapeutic view of redemption—that was needed in her fourteenth-century context, and that is needed for evangelism today.[31] Because of the intellectual and spiritual consequences of the fall, Julian notes, it is easy for Christians to believe in God's power,[32] but hard for them to believe in God's love.[33] That is, belief in God's almightiness without trust in God's love leads Christians to fixate on sin and the judgment of God, toward themselves and others. Out of this juridical worldview comes the kind of "evangelistic" message that perverts the good news of salvation into threats of hellfire and damnation and presents a bloodthirsty, tyrannical God.[34] Hamartiology in this case focuses on

29. Ibid., 137, 148, 166, 198, 225.
30. Ibid., 281.
31. Unlike the early church, which looked forward to the parousia because of confidence in *Christus Victor*, the one who overthrows the power of Satan, the medieval church was essentially fearful of Christ the Judge. The overthrow of evil meant the condemnation of *sinners*. See Zachary Hayes, *Visions of a Future*, New Theology Studies 8, ed. Peter C. Phan (Collegeville, MN: Liturgical Press, 1989), 168. In the same way Julian's mystical theology can provide a corrective to excessive legalism in some parts of the conservative church today. See Thompson, *Christology and Spirituality*, 126.
32. That is, God's omniscience, omnipotence, and omnipresence.
33. Julian of Norwich, *Showings*, 323. Here she is addressing the common error in her day in which God's power is seen overwhelmingly in terms of wrathful judgment, rather than God's all-powerful love. Julian's emphasis is helpful in contemporary questions of theodicy, in that her emphasis is on the re-creating power of God that overcomes all evil and brings forth life from death.
34. Brian D. McLaren laments that evangelism is a word "so bastardized that I can hardly bear to use it," even though he considers his primary ministry to be evangelism (*More Ready Than You Realize: Evangelism as Dance in the Postmodern Matrix* [Grand Rapids: Zondervan, 2002], 12).

sinners, with virtually no attention to those who are sinned against. All this is turned on its head by Julian's vision of God. Wounds precede sin—original wounds—and for this reason the eyes of the Lord look upon the human predicament "with pity and not with blame."

Julian's doctrine of the healing, transforming mercy of God is unsurpassed in holding forth hope to people with all forms of brokenness, which must be a central concern for evangelism. Within and beyond the Servant Parable, Julian's theology abounds with healing images: Christ as our clothing, our safe place, our strong and tender Mother. In the midst of suffering and sin, brokenness and alienation, Julian sees that humanity is God's bliss, God's reward, God's honor, and God's crown.[35]

Love is God's meaning. Julian sees the mighty power, the absolute authority of the Lord. Yet the Lord of her vision exercises authority by means of kenosis. His power is life-giving, maternal, fiercely set on the liberation of captive souls. When Jesus comes a second time it will be to perform a "great deed," not of damnation but of redemption. Julian cannot say when or how God will do this, but she is quite certain that all will be well.

Hans Urs von Balthasar's Hope for the World

The hope in God's love that Julian communicates through one book, *Showings*, Hans Urs von Balthasar (1905–1988) expounds in his astonishing corpus of more than one hundred books and hundreds of articles. Today Balthasar attracts increasing, well-deserved attention among theologians from all major Christian traditions: Catholic, Orthodox, and Protestant. During his lifetime, however, Balthasar's theology was less than enthusiastically received by many of his peers. The problem was that he consistently marched to his own theological drummer, in some ways anticipating a methodology that would speak to postmoderns.[36]

---

35. Julian of Norwich, *Showings*, 216.

36. Moss and Oakes comment, "Balthasar has more or less single-handedly heaved up a huge mountain range of theology, one that perhaps cannot be ignored as if it did not exist but certainly can be dismissed as *sui generis* and personally idiosyncratic" (Edward T. Oakes and David Moss, eds., *The Cambridge Companion to Hans Urs von Balthasar* [Cambridge: Cambridge University Press, 2004], 2, 13). Mark McIntosh describes Balthasar's work as "mystagogical," a genre that integrates analysis with

Edward T. Oakes and David Moss note, "One reason for Balthasar's relative isolation—perhaps even alienation—from the guild of professional
theologians is that he does not come out of, or represent, a *prior* school
of thought. Except, of course, his own."[37] The Swiss theologian defies
categorization, and with a spirit reminiscent of John Wesley, drinks from
wells across and beyond his own Catholic tradition so that his thought
resonates with diverse themes in Orthodox, Protestant, and Catholic
traditions.[38] His deepest concern is always the connection of men and
women with the meaning of the gospel revealed in Jesus Christ.

Neither liberal nor conservative, Balthasar was, at heart, a mystic.
What is central, most creative, and controversial about Balthasar's
theology is his eschatological vision.[39] Compelled by a trinitarian
understanding of God's kenotic love, Balthasar defines God's omnipotence as the way in which God loves. Love is God's meaning, so
that every attribute of God must be understood in terms of kenosis—
the divine, self-giving love of Father, Son, and Holy Spirit. Humans
can be whole and fully alive only as we join in with the Triune God's
kenotic, salvific mission in this world.

In his tightly compacted *Credo*, written shortly before his death,
Balthasar explains that God's "almightiness" refers to God's "un-
limited and free power to surrender" in self-giving love for the sake
of the world.[40] The Son is the "realized love-almightiness of the

---

the invitation to transformation and that takes seriously the lives and writings of the
saints and mystics as primary sources for theology. Balthasar and Karl Rahner are
two twentieth-century theologians highlighted by McIntosh for their integration of
theology and spirituality (McIntosh, *Mystical Theology*, 90–118).

37. Oakes and Moss, *The Cambridge Companion*, 2.

38. In regard to ecumenism, Balthasar writes that "ecumenical dialogue can bear
fruit only if it seizes on what is most deeply Christian and, faithful to its utter seriousness, develops a sense for what is secondary and relative, for what therefore can
be conceded on both sides." He also critiques the trajectory of liberal theology for
its increasing dilution of the claims and "the troublesome formality of the name"
of Jesus (Hans Urs von Balthasar, *My Work: In Retrospect* [San Francisco: Ignatius
Press, 1993], 56–57).

39. Balthasar, *My Work*, 25; Geoffrey Wainwright, "Eschatology," in *The Cambridge Companion*, 113.

40. Hans Urs von Balthasar, *Credo*, Introduction by Medard Kehl, trans. David
Kipp (New York: Crossroad, 1990), 31. Kehl observes that *Credo* is actually a "little
summa" of Balthasar's thought, distilling the most important themes of all his writing, in this short discussion of the Apostles' Creed (7).

Father."[41] Balthasar argues for the power of love expressed through the essential quality of surrender, of giving oneself up for that which is loved. Out of God's infinite will and ability to give, Christ came to earth, died, and descended into hell where God's love was finally and most fully revealed. There, in hell, Balthasar argues, Jesus experienced a dark night unlike any the world can ever know. He not only carried sin in solidarity with humankind, but literally became sin for us so that we can become the righteousness of God.[42]

Rejecting every theory of substitutionary atonement that is punitive, Balthasar presents a doctrine of atonement in which Jesus, out of loving solidarity with humanity, willingly bears humanity's sin and despair, our godforsakenness.[43] Jesus does this in his body, mind, and spirit, not wanting to avoid any aspect of suffering that humanity suffers. As seen in Julian's vision, Jesus would gladly suffer more for us if it could help us in any way. Having suffered death and hell with and for humanity, in his resurrection Jesus gathers up the dead and "takes them along"[44] into life. Salvation is thus offered to the whole world, with Jesus's death and resurrection efficacious for all.

God's "almightiness" is revealed yet again as evangelistic grace reaching out to sinners. Omnipotence in this instance means God's ability to "exert influence on human hearts without overpowering them. . . . Enticing forth from them, through the mysterious power of grace, their free assent to the truly good."[45] Thus God is able to work in mysterious ways that neither "break nor neutralize" human freedom, yet are able to "outwit" the blindness of fallen humanity in its resistance to the love of God.[46]

41. Balthasar, *Credo*, 69.

42. Ibid., 52.

43. For a clear, concise summary of Balthasar's critique of several models of atonement from the fathers through Luther and into the twentieth century, with Balthasar's own model, see Antoine Birot, "God in Christ, Reconciling the World to Himself: Redemption in Balthasar," *Communio: International Catholic Review* 24 (Summer 1997): 259–85.

44. Balthasar, *Credo*, 59.

45. Ibid., 65. Here, Balthasar's theology bears some resemblance to Wesley's doctrine of prevenient grace, and to the Eastern doctrine of *theosis*.

46. Balthasar firmly rejects double predestination, contending throughout his work for genuine free will of humanity as part of what it means to be made in the image of God. For God's love that outwits human resistance, see Hans Urs von Balthasar, *Dare*

Balthasar carefully spells out, again and again, his premise that Christians ought to hope for the salvation of all people, because God hopes for all people.[47] He is clear that hell is a real possibility for people and that we must guard against presumption as to who is and who is not saved. Yet the very heart of the gospel is love for one's enemies, which must of necessity include hoping and praying for their salvation. To do otherwise is to miss the meaning of the good news.[48] To consign persons to hell, even in one's imagination, is to pervert the meaning of the gospel and to presume a judgment that belongs to Christ alone. Thus the truly Christian position is one of hoping and praying for the salvation of all persons, including the "worst sinners." The normal Christian life is one of evangelistic mission to all people.

Drawing from the Bible and the thought of Irenaeus, Origen, Gregory of Nyssa, Maximus the Confessor, numerous medieval mystics (especially Julian of Norwich), Karl Barth, and Adrienne von Speyr,[49] Balthasar demonstrates that a high Christology requires a hope for all people; otherwise we imply that the sufferings of Christ were insufficient, incapable of bringing about the possibility of salvation for all. In keeping with many of the medieval mystics and Orthodox theologians, Balthasar argues that God's mercy and justice are one and the same.[50] The One who judges the world is the One who died to save the world. Therein lies our hope.

We Hope That All Men Be Saved? With a Short Discourse on Hell (San Francisco: Ignatius Press, 1988), 220–21.

47. Ibid., 18–28.

48. Ibid., 87.

49. Adrienne von Speyr, a Swiss physician who came to Balthasar for spiritual direction, was a modern mystic whose influence on Balthasar has been the cause for some of the "alienation" from his peers. The importance of their spiritual friendship was not unlike that of Teresa of Avila and John of the Cross, or Evelyn Underhill and Baron Friedrich von Hügel. Describing her role in the development of his own theology, Balthasar writes, "It was Adrienne von Speyr who showed the way in which Ignatius [of Loyola] is fulfilled by John [of the Cross] and therewith laid the basis for most of what I have published since 1940. Her work and mine are neither psychologically nor philologically to be separated: two halves of a single whole, which has as its center a unique foundation" (Balthasar, My Work, 89).

50. Ibid., 148–57. St. Isaac of Ninevah, for example, argues for the "scourge of love" as sinners experience the love of God after death. St. Catherine of Genoa, the subject of von Hügel's massive study The Mystical Element of Religion, offers a similar argument (Catherine of Genoa, Purgation and Purgatory: The Spiritual

Balthasar's overarching theological premise that love is God's meaning drives his ecclesiology and anthropology with their focus on "mission" as the highest purpose and meaning for human life. Commenting on the implications for Christian self-understanding in Balthasar's Christology, Mark McIntosh writes, "This is one of Balthasar's most central Christological motifs: obedience to the call of God not only turns out to make that calling present in the world but is the means by which the respondents become fully the true persons they were created to be."[51] Through embracing God's mission in this world, in other words, humans enter into the trinitarian life of self-giving love. Through the sanctifying work of the Holy Spirit, people are "initiated into the Mystery that God is love"[52] and empowered to love as Jesus loves, bringing the good news of the gospel into the world. Balthasar describes the life of discipleship as one of walking toward the eschaton, which "always involves *taking along* the *world*. Christ himself walked only in communion with others."[53]

In summary, Julian and Balthasar offer a model of atonement that takes seriously the presence of sin and evil in the world, as well as the righteousness of God's judgment, without being punitive. Unlike twentieth-century liberalism, which has generally rejected the doctrine of atonement, or the opposite end of the spectrum, which maintains a doctrine of atonement that is punitive, juridical, and fixated on the guilt of sinners, Julian and Balthasar point to an alternative portrayal of atonement in which God forgives our sin and heals the original wounds that led to sin. In this model, God the Father, Son, and Holy Spirit are all working together to bring about the healing of the cosmos. Their almightiness is revealed through kenosis. Neither Julian nor Balthasar deny the reality of hell or the possibility of hell for people. But fear of hell is not the motive for their evangelistic

---

Dialogue, Classics of Western Spirituality, trans. and notes by Serge Hughes [New York: Paulist Press, 1979]). According to this line of reasoning, God's judgment is reformative rather than retributive (Kallistos Ware, *The Inner Kingdom* [Crestwood, NY: St. Vladimir's Seminary Press, 2001], 206–9).

51. Mark A. McIntosh, "Christology," in *The Cambridge Companion*, 26–27.
52. Balthasar, *Credo*, 76.
53. Hans Urs von Balthasar, "Faith and the Expectation of an Imminent End," *Communio: International Catholic Review* 26 (Winter 1999): 696. Italics are in the original.

message. Instead, they offer a compassionate, profoundly hopeful vision of God's love that is healing, inclusive, and global, and that is concerned with individuals as well as communities, a perspective that is fundamental to a contemplative vision for evangelism.

How Original Wounds Lead to Sin: An Archetypal Reading of Genesis 1–3

To more clearly grasp the evangelistic ramifications of the premise of original wounds, let us take as a concrete example the original wounds of child sexual abuse. We will think about how the wounds happen, the consequences of the wounds, and the eventual bondage to sin that such wounds produce. I am using the example of child sexual abuse because it is paradigmatic of every other kind of original wound. Indeed, the narrative of child sexual abuse in our reflection on original wounds should be read together with the fall narrative of Genesis 3, which traditionally has been used to teach the doctrine of original sin.[54] In this reading[55] the narrative archetypically demonstrates how each of us moves from a position of blameless vulnerability as children toward becoming persons who are caught in a web of wounds and sin from which we cannot extract ourselves. Or to use the image from Julian's vision, it shows how the servant falls into the ravine.

54. My reading of this text has been shaped, in part, by Irenaeus's view of Adam and Eve as immature, childlike persons; Phyllis Trible's hermeneutic of the Bible (*Texts of Terror: Literary-Feminist Readings of Biblical Narratives* [London: SCM, 2002]) that honors the nameless, silent, and often maligned victims of violence in the Bible; and the many stories I have heard from survivors of sexual abuse. My reading of this text, with sexual abuse as the paradigmatic narrative of wounds leading to sin, does not exclude, diminish, or supersede the reality of other kinds of wounds and sin, including the sins of pride and self-will that have traditionally been linked to this narrative.

55. In the history of exegesis, these chapters have a multitude of interpretations (Claus Westermann, *Genesis 1–11* [Minneapolis: Augsburg, 1984], 186). Many of the interpretations include a commitment to the theme of sexual awakening or coming to sexual differentiation as Adam and Eve move from being "naked and unashamed" to fashioning clothing to cover their nakedness. See Susan Niditch, "Genesis," in *The Women's Bible Commentary*, ed. Carol A. Newsom and Sharon H. Ringe (Louisville: Westminster John Knox, 1998), 16. When read through the eyes of survivors of sexual abuse, there is far more to the story than sexual awakening.

When read in this way, the pathos of the human story unfolds wave upon wave, with the complex relationship between vulnerability, original wounds,[56] and sin far more apparent than is the case with what are so often superficial readings of the text, whether fundamentalist, wooden literalism, or a dismissal of the text as mere etiological myth.

This reading especially helps us to remember what Howard Thurman calls "the total fact" of a wounded person, who is much more than his or her brokenness and sin, but who has been irrevocably marked by it.[57] For if we can glimpse the incomprehensible webs of wounds, sin, and being harassed and helpless, we will be able to see through the eyes of Julian, who said that God looks at us "with pity and not with blame." We will understand why Balthasar urges hope for the salvation of even the worst sinner.

Before the fall, Adam and Eve are like children, naked and unashamed, playful and free in the garden of God's provision. They live in community with each other and God, a perichoretic relationship that images their Triune Creator. The only boundary given for them, according to the text, is the tree of knowledge of good and evil.[58] They are not to eat of its fruit, God warns, or they will die. Adam and Eve cannot know what "die" means, because they have not eaten of the tree. To know is to participate, and they have not "known" evil. For an unspecified amount of time, they leave the tree alone. They

---

56. Benedict J. Groeschel offers a pastoral hermeneutic of Genesis 3, calling original sin the "original wound," but despite his use of the word "wound" he remains committed to the concept of original sin as handed on from Augustine, with Adam and Eve as the first parents who "deliberately disobeyed God" (Benedict J. Groeschel, *Healing the Original Wound: Reflections on the Meaning of Salvation* [Cincinnati: Servant Publications, 1993], 22–24). On the contrary, Andrew Sung Park, along with Susan Nelson and others, has proposed the use of the Korean concept of "*han*" to interpret the way in which sin is passed from generation to generation. *Han* is the brokenheartedness, shame, bitterness, and other consequences that result from being sinned against. Thus Park's "original *han*" is much closer than is Groeschel's "original wound" to what I am proposing (Andrew Sung Park, *The Wounded Heart of God* [Nashville: Abingdon, 1993]; Andrew Sung Park and Susan L. Nelson, eds., *The Other Side of Sin* [Albany: State University of New York Press, 2001]).

57. Howard Thurman, "Mysticism and the Experience of Love," in *For the Inward Journey: The Writings of Howard Thurman*, ed. Anne Spencer Thurman (New York: Harcourt, Brace, and Jovanovich, 1984).

58. Gen. 2:9.

are blameless, naive, beautiful, and, like children, capable of being deceived. They are vulnerable, capable of being wounded.

Then one day one of the creatures speaks to them. God has not warned them to be suspicious of other creatures or to avoid the serpent. They have dominion over the creatures, including the serpent. The mystery of iniquity in the serpent is present, but its origin is unnamed in the text.[59] Like children, Adam and Eve are trusting of the familiar creature who shares the garden. They are unaware of the danger that lurks before them, so they listen vulnerably to the serpent's words. They do not "recognize" evil because they have not tasted evil, have not yet eaten of the forbidden tree.

As good parents we warn our children not to take candy from strangers and not to get into a car with a stranger. As good parents we may try to tell our children about good touch and bad touch, but they have no way of knowing what we're getting at, because they have not "eaten the fruit"; they have no capacity to imagine what we are warning them about. They are capable of being deceived, of being victimized by a familiar creature that has violence in its heart, candy in its hand, and a persuasive argument in its mouth. The serpent comes in the guise of Grandpa or Coach Miller or Aunt Sally. All children are vulnerable to deception and abuse. All children are Adam and Eve.

So, as the Scripture tells us, the serpent deceives Eve and Adam, who was with her. The text says that Eve saw that the fruit was delicious and beautiful. (Did she see the serpent take a bite, perhaps, without apparent consequence?) Wanting to be like the God she loved ("you will be like God, knowing good and evil"), promised a good outcome by the confusing but familiar creature she had no reason to fear, she accepted the fruit and gave some to Adam.[60] The primary way in which children are sexually abused is through an enticement

---

59. Walter Brueggemann comments that this narrative, along with the rest of the Old Testament, is not interested in questions about the origin of evil. Rather, the text is concerned "with faithful responses and effective coping" in a world in which evil exists (Walter Brueggemann, *Genesis* [Atlanta: John Knox, 1982], 41).

60. Westermann insightfully comments, regarding the nature of the temptation, that "at bottom what entices a person to transgress a limit is not the sensual pleasure heightened even more by the prohibition, but the new possibilities of life that are apparently opened by the transgression" (Westermann, *Genesis*, 249).

that they cannot understand, at the hands of a persuasive adult or older child whom they know and trust.[61]

What kind of disobedience was this, on the part of Adam and Eve? Was it pride and willful rebellion, as is so often claimed? Was it gullibility because Eve was easily duped as a woman, and shameful weakness on the part of Adam who should have known better than to follow his wife's foolish lead, as is traditionally presented? Or was it the disobedience of naive children who really cannot understand the enormity of their actions?

Adam and Eve cannot know how this event will forever change their future and the future of others. Theirs is the kind of "fall into a ravine" displayed by a vulnerable child who has been warned about strangers (don't take candy from strangers), but whose "stranger" turns out to be the uncle who deceives and violates her through sexual abuse. When Adam and Eve eat the proffered fruit, they swallow a pervasive shame that begins with their sexuality (they make loincloths) and extends to every part of life. Their precious freedom to trust God, each other, and themselves, and the wonderment and shalom between themselves and creation, are broken, and a sequence of death-dealing consequences is unleashed. No aspect of life is left untouched.

Alienation leading to violence has been released into their lives, part of the "death" that God had warned would happen if they ate the forbidden fruit. They could not have imagined the sorrow that would soon mark their lives. The consequences of their alienation would now include a male drive to dominate women, and women's struggle with enmeshment and fear.[62] Now Adam begins to define and control Eve, giving her the name "Eve" and no longer calling her Isha.[63] The original wound has become the source for oppression in the family. Sinful dynamics have been set in motion that will be handed

---

61. Rape Victim Advocacy Program, "Myths and Facts—Child Sexual Abuse," www.rvap.org/pages/myths_and_facts_about_child_sexual_abuse.

62. Patriarchy is thus the first systemic evil found in the Bible, emerging from original wounds.

63. When Adam first meets Eve in Gen. 2:23, he calls her "bone of my bone, flesh of my flesh" and names her Isha, the Hebrew word that sounds like Ish, the word for man, underscoring their equality. While "Eve" is a positive name, "mother of all the living," the former equality of the man and woman has been broken.

on to subsequent generations. Future violence of every kind, future
sin, begins with original wounds.

The story of Adam and Eve is the story of every person who has
suffered sexual abuse.[64] The shattering of trust leads to deep wounds
to the capacity for intimacy. Alienation, fear, and grief, the trauma
leading to brokenness of body, mind, and spirit, skew how survivors
see themselves, others, and the world. Images of God are deeply affected by the abuse. Out of distorted thoughts and beliefs, survivors
of sexual abuse develop a broad array of coping strategies to find
their way in life.[65] For some the patterns are around perfectionism in
an attempt to overcome the pervasive, deep-seated shame. For some
the wounds drive the attempt to control everyone and everything
in life in order to feel safe. For others the wounds drive addictions,
promiscuity, and a multitude of other destructive behaviors. Many
survivors of sexual abuse go on to a lifetime of relationships that are
abusive, dysfunctional, and chaotic, because of the residual effects of
the original wounds.[66] They are like Adam and Eve, toiling against

64. Again, let me remind readers that I am not saying that the "essence of sin"
is sexual abuse. To reiterate, child sexual abuse is paradigmatic for the process of
wounds leading to sin.

65. Many of these strategies are described in Dan B. Allender, *The Wounded Heart:
Hope for Adult Victims of Childhood Sexual Abuse* (Colorado Springs: Navpress,
1990). Park describes the residual effects of "disgrace shame" that is left in victims
of oppression, including sexual abuse victims, as disgust with the self, feelings of
deficiency, abandonment, defectiveness, and defilement (*Wounded Heart of God*,
83–84). For a related discussion of the pervasive effects of shame from child sexual
abuse from the perspective of moral philosophy, see Roger Scruton, *Sexual Desire: A
Moral Philosophy of the Erotic* (New York: Continuum, 1986), 295–98, 311–15.

66. At least one out of every three girls and one out of every six or seven boys in
the United States is sexually abused before the age of eighteen (FaithTrust Institute,
"Q&A," www.faithtrustinstitute.org). Many survivors do not understand how the
abuse has affected them until well into adult life, if ever. The effects of shame and its
origin in the abuse, for example, are not automatically clear to the survivor, so that
therapy of some kind is usually needed to help the survivor heal from shame. In describing childhood sexual abuse as paradigmatic of the manner in which wounds beget
bondage to sin, which is then handed on through wounds to others, I emphatically
am not saying that victims of sexual abuse automatically become sexual perpetrators.
Most survivors of childhood sexual abuse do not become sexual abusers as adults. The
wounds of sexual abuse do result in many kinds of attitudes and behaviors that then
become the source for additional wounding and sin, which may or may not be sexual.
For example, a survivor may become enslaved to sin against herself in allowing herself
to live in a relationship of domestic abuse as an adult. In all of this it is important

thorns, laboring at life, yearning for love and security. Like Adam and Eve hiding behind fig leaves, they do not perceive the actual love God has for them. They are the servant of Julian's parable, caught in a "narrow and comfortless place," suffering "seven" wounds, unable to see the face of the Lord who looks on them with infinite love.

The story of Adam and Eve is your story and my story in our loss of innocence and our wounding and our eventual bondage to sin. It is the universal narrative of original wounds. We have considered the example of child sexual abuse, but the paradigm is true for all forms of original wounds. Sin originates in wounds that come from living in this broken world. Regardless of the kinds of original wounds we receive, the mystery of iniquity is part of the world into which we are born. The world is already marked by sin, by death, and by evil. No life is untouched.

The marvelous good news in the midst of this universal tragedy is that love is God's meaning—toward Adam and Eve, toward every human. The promise of 1 Corinthians 15:22–28 is that wounds and sin do not have the last word. Love, not death, wins the day.[67] As Julian saw, "all manner of thing shall be well."

When we believe in and experience love as God's meaning, love becomes our meaning, for we become like the God we worship.[68] When love becomes our meaning, the ramifications for evangelism are

---

to keep in mind that victims of sexual abuse are not responsible for their abuse, and victims of domestic violence of any kind neither deserve nor cause the violence of their offenders. See Rape Victim Advocacy Program, "Myths and Facts—Child Sexual Abuse"; and the National Center for Victims of Crime, "Child Sexual Abuse," www .ncvc.org/ncvc/main.aspx?dbName=DocumentViewer&DocumentID=32315. For more about the sins of sexual abuse and domestic violence from a Christian perspective, see Carol J. Adams and Marie M. Fortune, eds., *Violence against Women and Children: A Christian Theological Sourcebook* (New York: Continuum, 1995). See also Allender, *The Wounded Heart.*

67. The "resurrection chapter" (1 Cor. 15) is the clearest biblical text supporting hope for the salvation of all people. See also Rom. 8:21, "the creation itself will be set free from its bondage to decay and will obtain the freedom of the glory of the children of God."

68. For a mischievous and theologically informed picture book about the relationship between God image and Christian self-understanding, especially in relationship to eschatology, see Dennis Linn, Sheila Fabricant Linn, Matthew Linn, and Francisco Miranda, *Good Goats: Healing Our Images of God* (New York: Paulist Press, 1993).

immense. We are cleansed of legalism, judgmentalism, coercion, and exploitation. We are liberated so that we can now see the "total fact" of others, which is so much more than their guilt and sin, or their wounds. This is not a sentimental, soft love. It is a tungsten power that respects others, says "no" to injustice, and unflinchingly involves itself in the muck and mire of broken lives. We can love in this way only because God first loves us. As those who gaze day by day into the eyes of the One who sees us "with pity and not with blame," we are changed. Our ecclesiology is changed—the stone rolls away from the tomb of the church and Christ strides out into the morning. Love is our meaning.

3

Broken Bread
and Poured Out Wine

To be people whose meaning is love is to become broken bread and poured out wine. It is about embracing holiness for the sake of the world. Holiness is a Godward posture, a complete belonging to God, a full commitment to the reign of God in this world, being set apart. Yet holiness is not a denial of one's own humanity. Nor is holiness a matter of "purifying" oneself by removing oneself from the muck and mire of actual life. On the contrary, the holy life is one that is fully engaged in this world in the name and power of Jesus Christ. As the lives of so many great saints and mystics demonstrate, the more one advances in the way of holiness, the more one must wrestle with "powers and principalities," for the same evil that opposed Jesus opposes those who live in the power of his name. Suffering of all kinds seems to mark the paths of many of the great saints and mystics, through illness, rejection at the hands of loved ones, persecution, and loss. But the light shines in the darkness, and the darkness will not overcome it. It is precisely in the midst of such adversity that these holy ones become testaments of divine love.

Two mystics who are exceptionally suited to interpret the way of holiness for our current situation are Phoebe Palmer, the lay Methodist preacher and theologian who became the mother of the nineteenth-century holiness movement, and an obscure Russian Orthodox hiero-monk,[1] Father Arseny, who spent some twenty years in Soviet death camps under Stalin's regime.[2] In the lives of these uncanonized saints we encounter the evangelistic power of holiness. Palmer's apophatic "altar theology" and Father Arseny's kenotic priesthood are exactly what the American church needs. They teach us how to live the daily martyrdom that is intrinsic to being "a royal priesthood, a holy nation, God's own people," so that we may, with integrity, proclaim the mighty acts of him who called us out of darkness into his marvelous light.[3]

Naked Faith in the Naked Word

It had been almost exactly one year since her baby died, Eliza's life snatched away in a tragic crib fire.[4] The loss nearly crushed Eliza's mother, Phoebe Palmer, who was still reeling from the deaths of two infant sons.[5] Would God also take her beloved husband, Walter, and their only living child? Had she loved them all too much? Were the children's deaths her fault because she idolized her family? These were

1. A hieromonk is an Orthodox monk who is also ordained as a priest and ap-pointed to serve outside the monastery.

2. The stories of Father Arseny are collected and translated in two volumes, Vera Bouteneff, ed., *Father Arseny: A Cloud of Witnesses* (Crestwood, NY: St. Vladimir's Seminary Press, 2001), hereafter known as *A Cloud of Witnesses*; and Vera Bouteneff, ed., *Father Arseny 1893–1973: Priest, Prisoner, Spiritual Father* (Crestwood, NY: St. Vladimir's Seminary Press, 2004), hereafter known as *Father Arseny*. For the value of hagiography toward shaping holiness of life, see Robert L. Wilken, *Remembering the Christian Past* (Grand Rapids: Eerdmans, 1995).

3. 1 Pet. 2:9.

4. Eliza was eleven months old when she died on July 29, 1836. The nurse who was tending Eliza attempted to refill an alcohol lamp while it was still lit, igniting the netting around the crib, which was immediately engulfed in flames. Hearing the cries from the next room, Palmer rushed into the nursery but it was too late. Eliza died in her arms (Richard Wheatley, ed., *The Life and Letters of Mrs. Phoebe Palmer* [1881; repr., New York: Garland Publishing, 1984], 30–32).

5. Alexander, her firstborn, died in 1829 at the age of nine months. Samuel was just seven weeks old when he died in 1831. As Thomas Oden notes, questions of theodicy fill Palmer's poetry during this period and later (Thomas C. Oden, ed., *Phoebe Palmer*, Sources of American Spirituality [New York: Paulist Press, 1988], 76–83).

the questions that troubled the depths of Palmer's soul.[6] The night that Eliza died, Palmer cried out to God, keening for her baby, shocked and appalled at the manner in which her little one perished. Palmer describes receiving assurance that "some great good" would result from this terrible tragedy.[7] But a year later this assurance did not assuage her growing anxiety that perhaps she might lose even Walter.

Palmer could scarcely remember a time when she had not known God.[8] From the age of four she earnestly sought to please the God she loved. She had grown up in a devout Methodist family, had always gone to church, and had never knowingly disobeyed her parents. Her marriage to Walter Palmer, a physician, was strong and loving. Yet the faith of her youth could barely sustain her burden of unanswered questions and grief. Try as she might, she could not feel the warmth, joy, or assurance, the presence of God that seemed the norm for everyone else. There was no assurance of being sanctified when she prayed prayers of consecration. It had always been the case that her faith was more rationalistic than affective, a reality that had troubled her often in the past.[9] But now the absence of feeling was oppressive.[10]

6. Phoebe Palmer, *Incidental Illustrations of the Economy of Salvation, Its Doctrines and Duties* (Boston: Henry V. Degen, 1855), selections republished as *Full Salvation: Its Doctrine and Duties* (Salem, OH: Schmul Publishing Co., n.d.), 145–46; Phoebe Palmer, *The Way of Holiness* (1843; repr., Salem, OH: Schmul Publishing Co., 1988), 151–52. Palmer's theological anxiety over having loved her children too much was part of her Methodist religious milieu. As Diane LeClerc notes, Wesley was ambivalent toward marriage and family life, because in his view family so easily became an idol in women's lives. According to LeClerc, he considered the idolatrous love of family as one form of original sin. His callous attitude toward his own sister's loss of her children is one of numerous examples (Diane LeClerc, *Holiness of Heart: Gender, Sin and Holiness in Historical Perspective* [Lanham, MD: Scarecrow, 2001], 68–71, 79, 83, 89–92, 113–15).

7. Wheatley, *Life and Letters*, 30–32.

8. For biographies of Phoebe Palmer see Harold E. Raser, *Phoebe Palmer: Her Life and Thought* (Lewiston, NY: Edwin Mellen, 1987); and Charles Edward White, *The Beauty of Holiness: Phoebe Palmer as Theologian, Revivalist, Feminist and Humanitarian* (Grand Rapids: Zondervan, 1986). For Palmer's journal entries and personal correspondence see Wheatley, *Life and Letters*.

9. She considered her rationalistic, deeply analytical mind to be more of a liability than an asset, and a source of temptation to doubt God (Palmer, *Way of Holiness*, 56–57, 87).

10. Palmer's description of her inability to feel is consistent with the emotional flatness of clinical depression. Given the grief she carried over the deaths of her children, depression may well have contributed to her spiritual dilemma.

So it was that on July 27, 1837, Palmer reached a crisis of faith. Battling through a series of eight temptations, Palmer made a contract with God, an irrevocable "altar covenant" in which she presented herself to God as a living sacrifice, given absolutely and unconditionally.[11] She offered to God her entire life with all its losses and unanswered questions, in order to enter the "way of holiness" and be about God's mission in the world.

As Palmer worked through the eight temptations, answering each one with Scripture, she came to see that she could trust the promises in the Bible, whether she emotionally felt anything or not. For Palmer, the Bible was the voice of the Holy Spirit.[12] Wrestling with the desire for an emotional manifestation that would prove she had been sanctified, Palmer sensed the Holy Spirit challenge her to believe the written word of God as quickly as she would believe an audible voice from heaven, telling her that she was sanctified.[13] The written word of God promised "I will receive you," therefore, Palmer reasoned, it was her duty and gift to believe this promise and begin to live as if it were true instead of waiting for some outward sign.[14] She agreed with God that she would "lay hold of the Word" in this promise and trust that she had been fully received and fully sanctified. Even if she never felt any religious emotion for the rest of her life, she wrote, she resolved to walk by faith and "hold on in the death struggle."[15] To demand an affective experience as proof of sanctification was tantamount to the sinful Pharisees demanding another sign in order to believe the words of Christ.[16] The contract was her way of expressing "naked faith in the naked word" of God, the culmination of her long, increasingly painful search for a spiritual *experience*. When she reached the point of

11. Palmer chronicles her day of days in several sources, including *Faith and Its Effects: Or Fragments from My Portfolio* (1854; repr., Salem, OH: Schmul Publishing Co., 1999), 43–54; *Way of Holiness*, 15–32. See also Oden, *Phoebe Palmer*, 114–22.

12. Palmer's reading of the Bible was informed by careful exegetical work, using the tools of Bible research that were available to her. The best example of her considerable hermeneutical skill is her landmark work on women's right to public ministry, *Promise of the Father* (1859; repr., Salem, OH: Schmul Publishing Co., n.d.).

13. Wheatley, *Life and Letters*, 40.

14. Ibid., 41.

15. Ibid.

16. Luke 11:29.

being willing to remain in an emotionally arid condition permanently, Palmer wrote, her covenant with God was finally consummated. She had fully surrendered herself to God.

Though she could not have known it on her day of days, Palmer was destined to become the mother of the nineteenth-century holiness movement. The apophatic nature of her day of days, with its "naked faith in the naked word" and its kenotic surrender of her life, would become the basis for her "altar theology" with its three parts of entire consecration, faith in God's word, and public witness to what God has done.[17] Palmer would indeed feel religious emotion in the future, including the profoundly healing assurance of God's love. She would come to experience the presence of God in numerous ways, including visions, dreams, and spiritual combat, and she would preach and teach with so much power that more than twenty-five thousand people would enter "the way of holiness" through her ministry.[18] Her impact on the world would equal that of Charles Finney,[19] and her legacy would be more than a dozen new holiness denominations. Numerous social justice endeavors would trace their beginnings to Palmer.[20] All of this was in her future, but on her day of days, all she knew for

17. These are best understood both as initiatory steps into sanctification and as simultaneous, ongoing processes, as Palmer makes clear in her teaching about the necessity of choosing to keep all on the altar day by day (Palmer, *Way of Holiness*, 87).

18. That is, they would be fully evangelized so that they, too, became committed to a fully surrendered life of holiness for the sake of the world. Many of them were church members whose faith was nominal to nonexistent, one of the hardest groups to evangelize (Tucker and Liefeld, *Daughters of the Church*, 263).

19. Ibid. Oden designates Palmer as the most significant Protestant female theologian in the history of the church due to the breadth and quantity of her writing; the exegetical, theologically precise, and practical nature of her work; and her contributions as a preacher, humanitarian, and protofeminist. He also assigns her as the pivotal figure in the transition between Methodism and Pentecostalism (Oden, *Phoebe Palmer*, 14–15, 16–19).

20. Palmer was a cofounder of Five Points Mission, the first Protestant settlement house in America, and also founded one of the first prison ministries in America. Together with her husband, Palmer was active in numerous outreach efforts to assist the poor and relocated her and her husband's church membership to a struggling community of the poor in the lower east side of Manhattan. Among Palmer's disciples who went on into significant social ministries were William and Catherine Booth, founders of the Salvation Army; Francis E. Willard, founder of the Women's Christian Temperance Union; and Amanda Berry Smith, a former slave who became a powerful international evangelist and humanitarian (Oden, *Phoebe Palmer*, 12).

certain was that she could no longer put anyone or anything before God. Nor could she demand a particular experience from God. Her life was to be one of naked faith in the naked word of God.

The Way of Father Arseny

A hundred years later on the other side of the world, a gaunt, prematurely aging priest rose from his prayers. Wrapping a flimsy cotton jacket more tightly around his lean frame, the man left the barracks to begin gathering wood for the day's fire. His head bowed against the cold wind, Father Arseny mouthed the words of the prayer that pulsed sanity through his days and nights: "Lord Jesus Christ, Son of God, have mercy on me, a sinner!"[21] Around him other prisoners moved into the gray morning with its monotony of hard labor, cruelty, and deprivation. The prisoners were a strange mixture of hardened criminals, clergy, intellectuals, and unfortunate government workers who found themselves labeled as political dissidents, sometimes for no reason other than spite at the hands of a jealous coworker. To all of them the priest—Prisoner No. 18376—gave himself day after day in prayer, friendship, and love. He was a contradiction to everything about the camp, a brightly shining beacon of hope, a divine smile penetrating the gloom of despair. Father Arseny was a living martyr, spending himself for the love of God in a maw of unfathomable suffering. Through his twenty years in the death camps and afterward, Father Arseny led countless people to deep and abiding faith. His means of evangelism were prayer and kenosis, a life of self-giving in which he bore the sorrows and burdens of others and loved them into the kingdom.[22] He was a living prayer.

Father Arseny was born in Moscow in 1894[23] and graduated from the Imperial University of Moscow with a degree in art history, spe-

21. Known as "the Jesus Prayer," the narrative of the development of this form of centering prayer is found in the anonymously authored classic, *The Way of a Pilgrim: And the Pilgrim Continues His Way*, trans. R. M. French (San Francisco: HarperSanFrancisco, 1991).

22. Bouteneff, *Father Arseny*, 137.

23. Names of individuals and exact dates for some events (including the dates for Father Arseny's birth and death) were changed in early editions of the text in order

cializing in Russian art and architecture. After graduating from the university and having published some of his work, Father Arseny went to the Optina Pustyn Monastery to consider a monastic vocation. In 1919 he was ordained as a hieromonk.[24]

Father Arseny, whose name means "courageous,"[25] was one of tens of thousands of Russian Orthodox Christians who were persecuted under the Soviet regime from 1924 until the fall of communism in 1991. Between 1924 and 1953, during the Stalin era, "six hundred bishops, forty thousand priests, and one hundred twenty thousand monks and nuns were killed," to say nothing of the thousands of faithful lay Christians who perished.[26] The persecution of Christians of all kinds did not stop with Stalin's death. As Kallistos Ware comments, the martyrdom of Soviet (and Ethiopian) Christians between 1974 and 1991 "makes the persecutions of the early church in the Roman Empire, even under Diocletian, appear relatively mild and humane."[27]

Father Arseny's first arrest took place in 1933. After his second arrest in 1939, he remained in various "special" camps[28] until 1958, when he was released. He lived the rest of his life in a small village, Rostov, where he was cared for by a former atheist and persecutor of Christians whom he had evangelized, Nadezhda Petrovna.[29] There he received visitors every day, "spiritual children" whom he had evangelized and to whom he provided ongoing spiritual direction.[30]

---

to protect the Orthodox community from further persecution. Thus Father Arseny's birthday is variously given as 1893, 1894, and "sometime in the first decade of the twentieth century" (Bouteneff, *Father Arseny*, viii). His gravestone is marked 1894–1975.

24. Bouteneff, *A Cloud of Witnesses*, 9.

25. Bouteneff, *Father Arseny*, 133.

26. Ibid., vi.

27. Ware, *Inner Kingdom*, 112. Kay Marshall Strom and Michele Rickett note that women often suffer the most under religious persecutions. For a collection of deeply moving narratives of contemporary Christian women who suffer persecution, see Kay Marshall Strom and Michele Rickett, *Daughters of Hope: Stories of Witness and Courage in the Face of Persecution* (Downers Grove, IL: InterVarsity, 2003).

28. "Special" camps were the most severe labor camps, with a very low survival rate for prisoners.

29. Bouteneff, *Father Arseny*, 102–6.

30. In the Orthodox tradition it is customary for persons to refer to those who spiritually lead and mentor them as spiritual fathers or mothers. This terminology underscores the deep love and commitment and sense of responsibility that are expected of spiritual fathers and mothers toward those in their care.

The Evangelistic Power of Kenosis

Through their personal crucibles of great suffering and loss, Phoebe Palmer and Father Arseny became holy people, developing the kenotic spirituality that was the source for their extraordinary power in ministry. There are many ways in which the American church needs the testimony of Palmer and Father Arseny. For the purpose of the discussion at hand, however, we will limit our focus to two points: Palmer's fundamentally apophatic approach to holiness and Father Arseny's kenotic understanding of priesthood.

What revolutionized Palmer's life was the profound paradigm shift that took place when she finally realized that God, not her experience of God, was the focus of holiness. This was a move from essentially kataphatic to apophatic spirituality. (Her crisis was generated in no small part by the absence of any kind of apophatic conceptual framework within her Methodist theology.)[31] Sanctification, she came to see, was not about her having particular emotional experiences or spiritual manifestations, nor was holiness essentially about following a checklist of rules governing behavior, appearance, and religious activity.[32] Holiness, Palmer realized, is about a life given irrevocably to God, which then in union with Christ the Sanctifier is empowered to be in God's redemptive mission in the world. As Palmer later taught hundreds of times in groups small and large, in books, and in letters of spiritual direction, Christ is the altar, and whatever touches the altar is made holy.[33] "The secret of power is union with Christ," Palmer wrote.[34]

31. This was a striking weakness in John Wesley's sanctification theology, with his emphasis on assurance (an "inner witness") of salvation and his aversion to all things apophatic.

32. The irony of this is that subsequent interpreters of Palmer's sanctification theology often attributed to Palmer the later development of rationalistic, legalistic theology that was overwhelmingly concerned with external rules and appearances.

33. Palmer's "altar theology" centers on two concepts: first, that the altar sanctifies the gift, and second, that Christ himself is the altar. As always, these convictions are based on Scripture. Palmer's understanding that the altar sanctifies the gift is based on Matt. 23:19, in which Jesus answers his critics with a quote from Exod. 29:37. The gift is not intrinsically holy; rather, the altar of sacrifice is what makes the gift holy (Palmer, *Way of Holiness*, 43). This is but one of many texts in which she makes this claim.

34. Palmer, *Full Salvation*, 55.

Palmer believed that the call to holiness was universal for every Christian, that it was the "normal" way of life for God's people. Holy Christians are, in her terminology, Bible Christians. Furthermore, she argued that unholy Christians—lukewarm, biblically illiterate professors—are the primary reason that the world is in such a sorry state and that so many people resist evangelism.[35] Like so many of the great reformers before and after her, Palmer preached that a return to the way of scriptural holiness was necessary so that the world could experience the evangelistic, embodied presence of Christ. Nothing less would do.[36]

Thus we find in Palmer's teaching and life a radical commitment to kenosis, a self-emptying love that serves a broken world. As already noted, a commitment to serving the poor led Phoebe and Walter to move their church membership from their comfortable middle-class Allen Street Church to a new church in an impoverished neighborhood near Five Points Mission.[37] Palmer was active in many social justice endeavors, including prison ministry, alcoholic rehabilitation efforts, and the care of orphans. Her poetry and correspondence reflect abolitionist convictions.[38] Even more striking was Palmer's commitment to defy patriarchal cultural norms, publicly teaching and preaching her message of scriptural holiness, bringing on herself the criticism and ridicule of many detractors. In all of these prophetic activities, Palmer's courage and stamina came from the power of the Holy Spirit, working in and through Palmer's surrendered life.

Palmer's apophatic theology of holiness played a central role in the way she faced and interpreted the many losses and struggles of her

35. For one of many texts in which this claim is made, see Palmer, *Way of Holiness*, 147.

36. Palmer's writing is filled with the teaching that the Bible is to be the supreme source of faith and practice for the Christian, that it has authority higher than any human authority or experience, and that it is the word of God. A "Bible Christian," in other words, is one who has submitted his or her life to the authority of the Bible and who is radically transformed by the internalization of the message of the Bible. This transformation is the work of the Holy Spirit, whose "voice" is Scripture (Palmer, *Full Salvation*, 31, 74; Palmer, *Way of Holiness*, 16–17, 28, 38, 52–53, 57, 79).

37. Oden, *Phoebe Palmer*, 12–13.

38. Ibid., 13, 83.

life.[39] The most agonizing of these, seeing her baby burn to death, was the most profound in its effect on Palmer's spirit. Crying out to God for solace in the face of such horror, Palmer sensed divine assurance that as she would carry out her ministry with the same love and devotion she had poured into Eliza, the result would be the evangelization of many people.[40] And that is indeed what happened as the years went by. So it was that Palmer embraced even the mystery of Eliza's death as a means of kenosis, giving to God not only the daughter she lost but a trustful commitment to love and serve God out of the emptiness of that loss. Everything she had, everything she was, everything she lost, she placed on the altar of Christ day after day, a living sacrifice, holy and acceptable to God. She became broken bread and poured out wine for the world.

Father Arseny, had he known Palmer, may have given her his highest compliment, calling her a "true ascetic," for she embodied the kenotic way of life that is central to Orthodox understandings of holiness.[41] Prayer and living for others were the foundation of Father Arseny's life.[42] One of the many situations in which Father Arseny's prayer brought life into a death-dealing situation was an experience in which he and a young prisoner, Alexei, were put in a punishment cell after Father Arseny stopped a criminal who was in the process of beating Alexei to death.

The cell was a space the size of a small closet, about six feet long and two feet wide, with a board instead of a bed.[43] The cell was unheated and, with subzero temperatures outside, death was virtually certain for the old priest and the badly beaten young man. As Alexei,

39. Throughout Palmer's life she faced many difficulties, including recurrent, painful physical illness, public ridicule from religious detractors, and intense spiritual warfare that she described in terms of wrestling against the enemy, inner anguish, and the like.

40. Wheatley, *Life and Letters*, 32.

41. Ware describes the kenotic ethos of martyrdom that permeates Orthodoxy as its missional vocation. The self-emptying of martyrdom is carried out not only in literal death but also in the daily practices of self-giving service and self-denying presence to the needs of others. Therefore the monastic life, marriage, and simply maintaining a faithful Christian witness in the world are all expressions of daily martyrdom (Ware, *Inner Kingdom,* 111, 113–23).

42. Bouteneff, *Father Arseny*, 123.

43. Ibid., 33.

a member of Komsomol, the communist youth organization, began to talk about their impending death, Father Arseny responded with the assertion that God was with them and had given them space in the punishment cell so that they could pray aloud without disturbance. For the next forty-eight hours Father Arseny stood and prayed aloud, and as he did so Alexei, moving in and out of consciousness, experienced a spiritual transformation. Through Father Arseny's prayer, both survived the ordeal, and when they emerged Alexei was a Christian.[44] The miracle of their survival was one of many signs and wonders that accompanied Father Arseny's faith.

Yet he was not spared unspeakable suffering and loss. No angel appeared in the night to release him from the camp. Again and again he was subjected to interrogations and beatings, to deprivations and punishments. He witnessed ongoing atrocities as prisoners were starved, tortured, buried alive, and shot. He recorded his own struggle against despair in the midst of so much darkness. Yet in all of this he continued to offer himself as God's priest in the world, emptying himself for the sake of others. As Palmer would have described it, Father Arseny kept putting himself on the altar of Christ, day after day, in the midst of the hellish camps. His guiding texts were Galatians 6:2, "Bear one another's burdens, and in this way you will fulfill the law of Christ," and Matthew 22:37–39, "You shall love the Lord your God with all your heart, and with all your soul, and with all your mind . . . [and you] shall love your neighbor as yourself."[45]

Just as Palmer believed that "bad professors" were the primary cause of unbelief in the world, Father Arseny blamed self-serving clergy for the fall of Russia to communism.[46] The kind of priests the police could always exploit were the ones who were eager to get ahead, driven by personal ambition and the temptations of power and personal comfort.[47] All such striving for self-advancement by the clergy was, in his view, the worst kind of sin, for it betrayed vulnerable

44. Ibid., 31–37.
45. Bouteneff, *A Cloud of Witnesses*, 109, 209.
46. Bouteneff, *Father Arseny*, 56.
47. Bouteneff, *A Cloud of Witnesses*, 100.

people into the hands of demonic forces.[48] The vocation of the priest, Father Arseny believed, is intrinsically kenotic, a daily martyrdom of intercession and service in order to bring spiritual children into the kingdom of God and nurture them to maturity. The vocation of the priest is to be a living, breathing prayer.

Both Palmer and Father Arseny believed that whatever came into their lives was by the hand of God, either directly or with God's permission. Each believed that their task as God's servant was to be a holy person in every context. They were convinced that if they lived faithfully, completely surrendered to God in whatever the day might bring, they would lead people into the light of Christ. For each of them the call to holiness involved significant loss and suffering, yet they were willing to embrace such a call because they had experienced the reality of God's love. They knew that love is God's meaning.

This is the message of holiness the church in America needs. Now more than ever, when so many pastors measure their success in numbers, buildings, and budgets, the church is starving for holy leadership. This kind of holiness offers a witness that doctrinal arguments will never provide. It is an evangelistic beacon that exposes, judges, and rejects all the false, exploitive, and manipulative forms of evangelism that have blighted the name of God's church. Holiness of heart and life is the language that proclaims the good news to every culture in all times. As seen in Phoebe Palmer and Father Arseny, genuine holiness is deeply attractive, inviting people into relationship with the One whose meaning is love.

48. Interestingly, Father Arseny refused to talk about dark powers and principalities and, when questioned about the subject, urged his questioners to focus on the love of God, the mother of God, and the lives of the saints. To dwell on demonic powers, in his view, is spiritually harmful. In the face of these powers Christians should pray and continue to surrender themselves to God's love and light (ibid., 207–8).

4

Coming Home to Love

As we consider the love, kenosis, and humility of the saints, the sheer power of their presence in the face of a daunting world, we cannot help but ask: How could seminaries better prepare pastors to lead us through the night? How could we cultivate in seminary students greater holiness, the inner light, the rugged perseverance they will need?[1] How could we help them to "center down" in Christ, to find freedom from the false self with its driving pride and fearful shame?[2] How could we empower them to stay the course amid ecclesiastical fiefdoms with their little kings and queens? What would enable them

1. While most pastors in America will not face the degree of religious persecution many saints and mystics experienced from the church (such as the imprisonment endured by John of the Cross), reforming pastors who lead congregations toward greater spiritual health suffer many things at the hands of the church. Many clergy who deal with conflict within the congregation believe they will not receive support or understanding from denominational officials, so they resign from ministry. This is especially true of young clergy, who say they were not prepared by seminary to lead congregations through necessary change. Most of the time clergy leave the ministry not over nationally reported theological issues, such as homosexuality or doctrine, but rather because of power struggles within the local congregation in the areas of worship, finances, or congregational renewal (John Dart, "Stressed Out: Why Pastors Leave," *The Christian Century* 120, no. 24 [November 29, 2003]: 8–9).

2. Centering down is the Quaker term for contemplative prayer.

to be in but not of that world? The answer is found in coming home to love.

To understand this more clearly, let us turn to the stories of two twentieth-century mystics whose greatest gifts emerged from their struggle to find their identity. The stories of Thomas R. Kelly and Henri Nouwen are not so different from many of our stories. These remarkably gifted men had normal human needs, their lives driven by a confusing mixture of sacred call and all-too-human ambition, genuine faith and crushing disappointments, and by a restless longing to feel at home. For Kelly and Nouwen, freedom and healing finally came through events they never would have chosen for themselves.

In Search of True Self

Thomas R. Kelly was born in 1893 to a devout evangelical Quaker family, beginning his journey immersed in the evangelical Quaker subculture of southwest Ohio.[3] But the ink had scarcely dried on his college diploma[4] when Kelly began to chafe at his evangelical identity. It was the beginning of two decades of spiritual and intellectual ambivalence, as he wrestled with divergent pulls between evangelical piety and traditional Quaker mysticism, missional concerns, and intellectual pursuits, the life of the mind and the deeps of the heart. Some of his dilemma was caused by matters beyond his control, including the onset of World War I. The deeper and more persistent issue, though, was Kelly's struggle to come home to himself. The problem surfaced during the years of his graduate work as Kelly moved from his sheltered origins into the larger world.

Influenced by the intellectual and spiritual charisma of his philosophy professor, Rufus Jones, Kelly changed his program from chemistry to philosophy during his first year of graduate studies at

3. For biographic information I am indebted to Kelly's former student and friend, T. Canby Jones, *Thomas R. Kelly As I Remember Him* (Wallingford, PA: Pendle Hill Publications, 1988), and to his colleague and friend Douglas V. Steere, "A Biographic Memoir," in *A Testament of Devotion*, by Thomas R. Kelly (New York: Harper & Brothers, 1941), 1–28.

4. Kelly's undergraduate work was in chemistry, in which he excelled. He graduated from Wilmington College in southwest Ohio in 1913.

Haverford College. Under Jones's gifted tutelage Kelly discovered the medieval Christian mystics, in addition to invigorating studies in philosophy.[5] To support himself Kelly taught at a nearby Quaker boarding school. Then, driven by a desire to do missions work in Japan and concern for the spiritual life of Quakers in America, he switched from philosophy to divinity studies, enrolling at Hartford Theological Seminary in 1916.

The onset of World War I interrupted Kelly's seminary program. Like many of his pacifist Quaker contemporaries, Kelly first worked in a canteen among US soldiers, followed by a YMCA post in England, where his job was to inspect German POW camps. After just a few months Kelly was sent home by the YMCA because of his perceived lack of patriotism as he befriended and came to deeply love the German people interned in the camps.[6] After returning to the United States Kelly decided that instead of ministry he would pursue a career in academia, so he finished his divinity studies with the goal of moving into a doctoral program. He was offered a scholarship to a PhD program at Hartford, but Kelly instead took a teaching post in philosophy and Bible at his old alma mater, Wilmington College. He and his new wife, Lael, hadn't been there long when Kelly began to resent what seemed to him to be an intellectually stifling atmosphere.[7] Two years later Kelly was back at Hartford, starting his PhD and working as a pastor in a nondenominational church.

Though by nature a warm, kind, and fun-loving man, the strain of intense academic work and his inner struggles began to take a toll. On the day of his oral defense for his PhD, Kelly experienced his first stress-induced breakdown. As he stood for his exam, Kelly's mind went blank, with confusion and amnesia so pronounced that he could not recall his own name.[8] Knowing that Kelly was more than capable of completing his oral defense, the faculty gave him a second opportunity to take the exam, which he passed, earning the PhD in 1924.

5. Rufus Jones was a scholar in both fields and helped Kelly to locate the origins of Quakerism in medieval Christian mysticism.

6. Jones, *Thomas R. Kelly*, 20–22.

7. Ibid., 22.

8. Kelly called these episodes "woozy spells," which continued to plague him as time went by (ibid., 23).

The next ten years were filled with numerous moves between teaching appointments, short-term missions work, and additional graduate studies, driven by spiritual restlessness and the yearning to make a name for himself. By 1930 Kelly had come to believe that if he could complete a second PhD in philosophy at Harvard, he would be able to secure a position at an elite Eastern university and all would be well. At this time he was on the faculty of Earlham College, an evangelical Quaker institution. The religious culture at Earlham felt oppressive to Kelly compared to what he had experienced on mission trips to Europe and during his years of graduate work. Kelly asked for and received a year's leave of absence so he could begin postdoctoral work at Harvard. One year turned into two as Kelly continued his studies at Harvard and replaced a professor at Wellesley College who was on sabbatical. He and Lael cherished the hope that another job would open so that they would not have to return to Earlham, but nothing was available.

After he returned to Earlham in 1934, Kelly diligently labored on with his second dissertation, but to his great disappointment he learned that Harvard would not allow him to earn a second PhD in philosophy because he already had one. Conflicted by warring desires for intellectual prestige and spiritual vitality,[9] Kelly was unable to reconcile the fragmentation and disappointments of his life. He fell into a debilitating depression. Scarcely able to function, for months he trudged to his classes unprepared and then stumbled home to bed.[10] When the depression gradually lifted, Kelly doggedly finished the second dissertation. Once again he tried to persuade Harvard to allow him to stand for an oral defense and once again they turned him down.

A faculty position was offered to him at the University of Hawaii and he gratefully took it to get away from Earlham. Yet he was soon disappointed there, too, with what he thought was less than rigorous scholarship.[11] By this time his frustration extended to Western philosophy in general because of its detached approach to knowledge. Excited by more holistic Asian perspectives on philosophy as

9. Ibid., 28.
10. Ibid.
11. Ibid.

enlightenment, Kelly threw himself into the study of Chinese and Indian thought. He continued to dream of making a name for himself as an intellectual.

The more Kelly focused on finding himself through academic achievements, the more fragmented he became.[12] His health deteriorated from the stress, with the onset of numerous symptoms including headaches, allergies, infections, and chronic fatigue. The worst of the symptoms were the episodes in which his mind went blank, he became confused, and he lost muscle coordination.[13] After a year in Hawaii he felt himself sinking toward another depression.

Then suddenly there was a breakthrough. Kelly was offered a position at Haverford, a college of the intellectual caliber that he sought. He and his family[14] moved to Philadelphia, thrilled to begin a new life there. A year later Kelly finally secured permission to make an oral defense at Harvard for a second PhD. It seemed that he would finally have everything he ever wanted, that all the moves, degrees, and sacrifices would pay off.

The oral defense was indeed a turning point in Kelly's life, but not in the way he had hoped. Instead, it was the event that both crushed him and set him free, for when he arrived for his oral defense he experienced yet another mental lapse with its amnesia, confusion, and physical symptoms. Unable to remember anything, he failed his oral defense. The Harvard faculty, having been resistant from the start toward Kelly's candidacy, told him he could never apply again for the degree.[15]

Utterly devastated by this failure, Kelly spiraled into a depression that was nearly suicidal. Humiliated by the staunch declarations he had made to his family and colleagues as to his true identity as a scholar and his determination to be a Harvard man, Kelly felt his life was over. He could scarcely imagine returning to Haverford to teach, even though his colleagues assured him that the Harvard experience

12. Alfred North Whitehead, under whom Kelly had studied during postdoctoral work at Harvard, commented to Kelly's wife, Lael, that Kelly was misguided in his pursuit of philosophy because his true passion lay in religion (ibid., 28).

13. Ibid.

14. By this time the Kelly family included two children, Lois and Richard.

15. Jones, *Thomas R. Kelly*, 30.

was irrelevant to his position there. They promised him that his failure
would be kept confidential.[16]

Then something completely unexpected took place. Kelly fell "into
the hands of the living God," where he was "wholly uprooted from
all earth-born securities and assurances" and overwhelmed with healing love.[17] His years of ambitious pride and frenetic activity were laid
bare in the presence of God. "Soul-shaking Love" invaded the depths
of Kelly's being, opening to him a contemplative vision of life lived
from the center.[18] He would never be the same, for in coming home
to the love of God Kelly had come home to himself. He references the
experience indirectly in several of his essays, describing the oceanic
love of God, holy fire, and the "Shekinah of the Soul."[19] Kelly emerged
from his depression radiant, with a spiritual power that shocked his
former colleagues at Earlham.[20]

Not long after the inner healing, Kelly made a trip to National
Socialist Germany in the summer of 1938. There he worked alongside German Quakers to help with the needs of many oppressed and
fearful people. Encountering human suffering of a magnitude he had
never experienced, Kelly was taken up again into the infinite love of
God, which rendered a deeper, childlike freedom.[21] He discovered
a depth of intercessory prayer that had been unprecedented in his
life along with a holy desire to minister to the "terrible wounds" of
the world.[22]

Kelly returned to the United States with a spiritual authority
that was palpable. Back at Haverford he gathered a small group
of students with whom he met for spiritual formation. Week by
week Kelly imparted to them the divine life that was being given

16. Ibid.
17. Thomas R. Kelly, *A Testament of Devotion* (New York: Harper & Brothers,
1941), 56–57.
18. Ibid. Coming home to the center for Kelly was much like it was for Augustine,
who wrote that his heart was restless until it found its rest in God.
19. Ibid., 29.
20. The word that they frequently used to describe the renewed Kelly and his
ministry was "authentic" (ibid., 24).
21. Jones, *Thomas R. Kelly*, 33.
22. Ibid. Indeed, prayer without ceasing and intercessory prayer are two of the
central themes in *A Testament of Devotion*.

to him. Kelly told his students that he wished they might become bands of itinerant preachers much like George Fox and the early Quakers.[23] Kelly now presided often at the required weekly chapel service at Haverford, where he ended nearly every message with an evangelistic call, urging listeners to surrender wholly to the One who is Love.[24]

The love of God had become a white-hot fire in Kelly. Gone were the restlessness and the ambition to make a name for himself. For three short years Kelly was a spiritual dynamo: speaking, writing, teaching, praying, and loving. When he died of a heart attack on January 17, 1941, he left a mystic's testimony of the unfathomable love of God. Virtually unknown for his work in philosophy, today Kelly is remembered for a handful of essays he penned on the spiritual life. Gathered mostly into a small book titled *A Testament of Devotion*, the meditations speak powerfully of giving oneself to God. Themes of simplicity, obedience, mission, and true community reveal a soul who had come home to himself.[25] With winsome humility Kelly names the "weasel-like" danger of spiritual pride, the "blurring of the soul's beauty" through moving too fast, and the mysterious power of intercession.[26] Kelly continues to call God's people to "center down," to find through contemplative prayer the self they were meant to be.[27] For too long, Kelly writes, God's people have been "prim and restrained."[28] The life to which we have been called is passionate, yet free from "strain and anxiety and hurry," a life that is unshakable because it has found its home in the love of God.[29]

23. Ibid., 38.
24. Jones reports that while a small group of "Tom's Boys" eagerly sat at his feet, a sizable number of arrogant, "self-styled intellectuals" mocked and ridiculed Kelly behind his back, calling him "St. Thomas" (ibid., 40).
25. For a helpful discussion of Kelly's spiritual theology, see Jerry R. Flora, "Searching for the Adequate Life: The Devotional Theology of Thomas R. Kelly," *Spirituality Today* 42, no. 1 (Spring 1990), available online at www.spiritualitytoday.org/spir2day/904214flora.html.
26. Kelly, *Testament of Devotion*, 62, 79, 108–9.
27. Ibid., 118–19.
28. Ibid., 119.
29. Ibid., 120.

First Love

Though coming from a Catholic tradition that in many ways is the polar opposite of Quakerism, Henri J. M. Nouwen was a contemplative in whom Thomas R. Kelly would have found a spiritual friend.[30] Nouwen's journey, like Kelly's, was marked with a pervasive restlessness as he struggled to come home to himself. Unlike Kelly, Nouwen was always certain of his priestly vocation. Nouwen was born in 1932 in Nijkerk, Holland, and knew from early childhood that he wanted to be a priest. His parents were both devout Catholics, and one of his uncles was a priest. As a young boy Nouwen loved to "play priest," complete with child-sized vestments, altar, and other liturgical items given to him by his grandmother. The family attic was even turned into a small chapel where young Henri enlisted family members to be his parish.[31]

Nouwen's journey into priesthood, the academy, and finally his work in the L'Arche community has been well-described in several biographies as well as in his own work.[32] Nouwen was one of the greatest spiritual writers of the twentieth century. His penetrating yet simple prose belies the intellectual stature of this brilliant, emotionally complex man. After his ordination to the priesthood in 1957, Nouwen completed graduate degrees in psychology and theology,[33] forging an

30. Traditional Quakerism is nonsacramental, nonliturgical, nondogmatic, and egalitarian.

31. Jurjen Beumer, *Henri Nouwen: A Restless Seeking for God*, trans. David E. Schlaver and Nancy Forest-Flier (New York: Crossroad, 1997), 13–19.

32. In addition to Beumer's biography, see Michael O'Laughlin, *God's Beloved: A Spiritual Biography of Henri Nouwen* (Maryknoll, NY: Orbis, 2004); and Michael Ford, *Wounded Prophet* (New York: Doubleday, 1999). While Ford's biography is the most thorough in some ways, it fails to capture the actual spirit of Nouwen. O'Laughlin's text provides a needed corrective, more fully contextualizing and normalizing Nouwen's personality and life's work in the manner he deserves. All of Nouwen's work is autobiographical, but especially so are his published journals, including *Spiritual Journals* (New York: Continuum, 1999); *The Inner Voice of Love: The Journey through Anguish to Freedom* (New York: Doubleday, 1996); and *Sabbatical Journey: The Diary of His Final Year* (New York: Crossroad, 1998). A wealth of resources are available through the Henri Nouwen Society at www.henrinouwen.org.

33. In both cases Nouwen's doctoral theses were rejected by the University of Nijmegen for not being scholarly enough. Instead of receiving a PhD in each discipline, he earned two professional degrees of *doctorandus* in psychology and theology (O'Laughlin, *God's Beloved*, 47, 53). In contrast to Kelly, Nouwen had no ambition

integrative approach that was unprecedented in his day and bore much fruit in the years to come. He taught pastoral theology at prestigious institutions, including Harvard and Yale, and published dozens of books on the spiritual life. He was an electrifying teacher and compassionate priest, a wonderfully artistic, lovable man, yet throughout his life he struggled with deep loneliness, a sense of unworthiness, and a fear of rejection. Nouwen could scarcely believe he was loved. He was in some ways a bundle of contradictions, a paradox of immense contemplative depth and startling insecurity. Life was a constant, anguished struggle to find his spiritual home. Out of this restless seeking Nouwen wrote the universal journey of the human heart.

The turning point came for Nouwen after he left Harvard in 1986 to become a priest at L'Arche Daybreak, a small community of mentally and physically challenged adults outside Toronto, Ontario. The decision came after protracted prayer and consultation with trusted friends, but it was a controversial choice. By that time Nouwen had become an international author and speaker whose books brought consolation and direction to countless people. He was a gifted ecumenist who interpreted the Christian message in a way that transcended all denominational barriers, speaking with equal power to evangelicals, Catholics, and mainline Christians, as well as persons of other faiths. His integrative work in psychology and theology had helped to open theological institutions to a new field, pastoral counseling.

After arriving at L'Arche, Nouwen found himself for the first time in his life in a community of people who did not know who he was and who could not be impressed with anything he had done. They could connect with Nouwen only in the way they connected with anyone else. He describes the experience as the most important one of his life, because it led him to discover his true identity through being his "vulnerable" self.[34]

Through becoming a beloved member of this community where he did not have to prove anything, Nouwen was finally opened to his deepest inner pain. He saw the many ways in which he had lived for

---

to make a name for himself in the academy and never felt entirely comfortable during his years at Yale and Harvard.

34. Henri J. M. Nouwen, *In the Name of Jesus: Reflections on Christian Leadership* (New York: Crossroad, 1992), 16.

the approval of others, seeking his identity in their affirmation. He came to see how he had lived entirely from his roles of priest, author, and teacher, disconnected in many ways from his own humanity. Then when his closest friendship fell apart, Nouwen experienced a complete emotional breakdown.[35] It was to become the most difficult experience of his life.[36] To receive the intensive therapy and safety he needed for recovery, he left L'Arche for several months to stay with friends who stood by him through his recovery.[37]

Through months of therapy and agonizing grief, Nouwen kept a journal. He wrote daily "imperatives" to himself after his therapy sessions, helping him to process what was happening and gradually to heal from the depression. After he returned to L'Arche, the journal was kept a secret, known only to his closest friends. Finally, after eight years and at their repeated urging, Nouwen agreed to publish it, hoping it would help others find healing and peace. *The Inner Voice of Love* contains the profoundly moving reflections of one whose greatest temptation in life was to doubt that he was loved.[38] What Nouwen came to deeply trust and what ultimately brought healing to his soul was what he calls the "first love" of God. Out of that love, Nouwen came to know his true self.[39]

God's "first love" reached out to both Thomas R. Kelly and Henri Nouwen in the center of their depression, penetrating the defenses and limitations of their carefully constructed selves, melting ambition, and calling forth the true beauty that was hidden beneath much fear. Out of their experience of coming home to God's love, each of them was released to fully give themselves to the world. Their legacy in spiritual writing includes some of the most compelling evangelistic texts ever penned.[40] More than anything else, they draw people to Jesus.

35. The friendship was with Nathan Ball, another assistant at L'Arche. The "interruption" of the friendship resulted from the strain of Nouwen's emotional fragility at the time. Eventually Nouwen and Ball were able to rebuild their friendship (O'Laughlin, *God's Beloved*, 75).

36. Nouwen, *Inner Voice of Love*, xiii.

37. Ford, *Wounded Prophet*, 165–67.

38. O'Laughlin, *God's Beloved*, 149.

39. Nouwen, *Inner Voice of Love*, 29.

40. Nouwen's finest work is one of his last books (*The Return of the Prodigal Son* [New York: Image, 1994]), a meditation on Rembrandt's masterpiece "The Return

Pedagogy of the Soul

The church in the night has lost much of its power to draw people to Jesus, thus the preparation of clergy for the night is of the greatest importance. Theological formation, the cultivation of holiness in our leaders, requires something far deeper than intellectual rigor, though rigor cannot be left behind. It must be pedagogy of the soul. It needs to be an Outward Bound[41] of the spirit, preparing sojourners for the rugged wilds.

The church in the night is a wilderness. It suffers from *Zerrissenheit*, "torn-to-pieces-hood,"[42] the spiritual fragmentation of inauthentic being. The church is harassed and helpless, in need of pastors who will live and move and have their being in what Kelly called the Infinite Center.[43] But the pastor is often the most torn-to-pieces of all, frenetic, striving, trying to be all things to all people, timidly avoiding conflict or angrily stirring it up, restless and unhappy, living a surface life. Many pastors have told me they rarely ever pray. There simply isn't time, they say, their eyes betraying the hunger of their souls. Their inner world is one that Kelly called a "whole committee of selves," each clamoring for its own mutinous demands.[44] The one thing necessary is a Divine Center, calling the scattered self into an integrated whole.

Yet life lived from the center is not without peril, for it is a call to come to die. The false self, that self that we craft in our own image, must give way to the self God calls us to be.[45] It must yield the throne

---

of the Prodigal." In this book Nouwen reflects on the call to become like the father in the story of the prodigal son, welcoming with open arms and unconditional love all who have wandered astray.

41. Outward Bound provides "character development and self-discovery" through a broad array of wilderness experiences and adventure trips. See "About Outward Bound," www.outwardbound.org.

42. Citing William James, Anne Morrow Lindbergh uses the term in her discussion of a woman's journey from being driven by others' demands to becoming an authentic self. The church is in many ways like the women Lindbergh references with this term (Anne Morrow Lindbergh, *Gift from the Sea* [New York: Vintage, 1978], 56).

43. Kelly, *Testament of Devotion*, 116.

44. Ibid., 114–15.

45. Thomas Keating, *Open Mind, Open Heart: The Contemplative Dimension of the Gospel* (New York: Continuum, 1995), 146.

to the One who is love. This is what Jesus meant when he said that we must die that we might live. He was talking about the false self.[46]

The false self is universal to the human experience, arising from wounds received in life. Overwhelmingly focused on production, performance, and making the desired impression on others, the false self constructs self-protective armor.[47] The false self confuses identity with function, so that we think we are what we do. The false self is a Pelagian who believes that everything is on his or her own shoulders. Love, for the false self, is always conditional. Driven by the false self, life is haunted with fear. Peace eludes us as we must continually be vigilant against failure or being found out. Woven through the fear is shame.

When we come home to the love of God everything changes, beginning with how we pray. Prayer is now at its foundation a contemplative soaking in the infinite love of God. All our intercessions and thanksgivings and wordless cries now issue from the molten core of contemplative prayer. Prayer has become the vital breath, the heartbeat of divine energy without which we cannot live. The deep security of being safely held, the comfort of our Anchor, the assurance of direction all come from this kind of prayer. The old pretensions and demands, the anxieties of the false self, become clear in the light of God's day, and our true call and true gifts, our true vocation, beckon to us with joy. We discover to our astonishment the truth of Jesus's words that his yoke is easy and his burden is light. Without realizing it we have entered the life of prayer without ceasing. Wonder of wonders, we know who we are and we know that we are loved. Coming to believe the truth of our own belovedness[48] leads to seeing others with new eyes. We become discerning, wise as serpents and innocent as doves. Indeed we are in but not of the world.

The minister of the future, Nouwen wrote, must be a mystic, one "whose identity is deeply rooted in God's first love."[49] Those who would lead us through the night must be schooled in contemplative

46. M. Basil Pennington, *True Self, False Self* (New York: Crossroad, 2000), 36.
47. Ibid., 35.
48. One of Nouwen's most beautiful books that focuses on accepting our essential belovedness is *Life of the Beloved* (New York: Crossroad, 1992).
49. Nouwen, *In the Name of Jesus*, 28.

prayer, for they can give only what they have received. Coming home to God's first love, they will come home to their true selves. Then they will know how to lead us toward heaven and will help us see how to live so that God's will "is done on earth as it is in heaven." The call to give ourselves in ministry is first and always a call to come home to love.

5

Healing the Threefold Wound

Julia's mother was a young woman when she refused "to submit herself" to her master.[1] As a result of her refusal, the master tied up Julia's mother and whipped her mercilessly. He then poured salt water over her bleeding wounds, adding to her torture. A week later when she was ordered to remove her dried, blood-soaked garment she could not do so because it was stuck to her lacerated flesh. The master's wife then ripped the "rough tow-linen undergarment" from her, tearing the skin off her back at the same time.[2] This and many other episodes of violence and degradation marked the life of Julia's

1. Julia Foote, "A Brand Plucked from the Fire: An Autobiographical Sketch," in *Sisters in the Spirit: Three Black Women's Autobiographies of the Nineteenth Century*, ed. and with an introduction by William Andrews (Bloomington, IN: Indiana University Press, 1986), 166. Foote's nuanced language suggests that the demand from the master may have been sexual, an everyday occurrence for many slave women and girls. For the sexual abuse of Native American women and girls by Christian colonizers, see Andy Smith, "Christian Conquest and the Sexual Colonization of Native Women," in *Violence against Women and Children: A Christian Theological Sourcebook*, ed. Carole J. Adams and Marie M. Fortune (New York: Continuum, 1995), 377–403.

2. Foote, "A Brand Plucked from the Fire," 166.

parents before her father was finally able to buy freedom for himself, then for his wife and infant.[3]

Julia Foote[4] was born free, but from financial necessity was sent at age ten to serve as a live-in domestic worker in the home of Mr. and Mrs. Prime, who lived not far from Foote's parents. At first she felt welcome and had affectionate feelings for the Primes, but that changed the day she was falsely accused of stealing pound cakes and received a brutal whipping from Mrs. Prime. Determined to force a confession from Julia, Mrs. Prime "wore herself out" on Foote, then promised another whipping for the next day until Foote confessed to the theft.[5] When Mrs. Prime left later that day, Foote secretly took the rawhide that had been used to whip her and chopped it to pieces with an axe.

Years later Foote learned that her mother "spoke sharply" to the Primes when they came to retrieve the frightened girl, who had run home to tell her mother of the injustice. One can only imagine the impact of the child's story on her mother, in light of her mother's experiences of violence. Even so, Foote had to return to the Primes' home, where she lived and worked until she was twelve. Although there was never another episode of abuse at their hands, Foote described the whipping as the event that hardened her heart against both the Primes and God. From then until her conversion, she considered herself a "hardened sinner."[6] Like many survivors of abuse, Foote's perceptions of and relationship with God were damaged by the violence. The "hardening of her heart" against God is the kind of response many survivors of sexual and domestic violence feel when their perpetrators receive the institutional support (or apathy) of the church.[7]

But at age fifteen, Foote's heart opened to God while she listened to a preacher at the quarterly conference of the African Methodist Episcopal Zion Church. The power of the Holy Spirit came upon

3. Ibid.
4. Julia Foote (1823–1901), was born in Schenectady, New York, the fourth daughter of freed slaves.
5. Foote, "A Brand Plucked from the Fire," 175–76.
6. Ibid., 176, 180–81.
7. For a helpful resource for spiritual healing in which survivors name their fears and distorted ideas about God in prayer, see Catherine J. Foote, *Survivor Prayers: Talking with God about Childhood Sexual Abuse* (Louisville: Westminster John Knox, 1994).

her, she reports, so that she fell unconscious and was carried home by others. While unconscious she saw and heard the redeemed singing of the others' salvation, yet she herself walked in spiritual darkness. She heard someone following her, telling her that she was bound for hell. Frightened and lonely, Foote cried out to God for mercy, longing to be redeemed. At that moment the taunting voice ceased, she understood the words of the songs of the redeemed and saw light. She awoke, "sprang from her bed," and began to tell everyone she had been redeemed.[8] Her conversion, like that of St. Paul, took place during a visionary experience.

Foote went on to become a powerful evangelist whose call to ministry also came through mystical visions and dreams. Like Phoebe Palmer, whose holiness theology influenced her, Foote experienced spiritual warfare with Satan, who mocked her and tempted her to disbelieve God and to doubt her own experience.[9] Yet in the same manner in which Palmer refuted Satan, Foote immersed herself in the Bible and prayer to resist the devil. Through the spiritual guidance of a woman whom Foote called "a mother in Israel," she came to experience sanctification. A number of kataphatic phenomena were involved in her reception of the Holy Spirit, including a sense of the "weight of glory" so heavy that it nearly pressed her to the ground. Perhaps the most important was the permanent removal of her previous fear of testifying to others about God.[10]

Ironically, some time later when God called Foote to preach she struggled mightily, because she didn't believe that women should preach.[11] The call was clear and strong, coming to Foote in a vision, but for two months Foote shrank back. Finally, she reports, she had a profound encounter with the Holy Trinity,[12] one that sealed forever her call to ministry and how she saw herself as a woman, an African-American, and a preacher of the gospel.

8. Foote, "A Brand Plucked from the Fire," 180–81.
9. Ibid.
10. Ibid., 182–86.
11. Ibid., 200–201.
12. It is not uncommon among nineteenth-century holiness women's descriptions of their mystical experiences for them to record experiencing the Father, Son, and Spirit as separate and distinct persons during prayer, visions, and so on. This is true of many mystics throughout Christian history, including Julian of Norwich.

A Trinitarian Call to Ministry

The vision was multisensory, including sight, sound, touch, taste, and smell. It lasted for many hours, beginning during a time of fervent prayer on a Sabbath evening. An angel came and led Foote to the Father, Son, and Holy Spirit beneath a massive tree. Many others were there as well, but she could not tell whether they were angels or people. God the Father told her she must make her choice about answering her call, warning her of eternal suffering if she refused. When she remained silent, God took her hand. Foote thought she was going to be led to hell, so she cried out that she would obey God and go anywhere God led her. God then pointed in many directions, each time asking if she would go there. To each question she answered, "Yes."

After that God led her to the edge of a great sea, where he brought her to Christ. There she experienced an extraordinary cleansing, healing, and commissioning that was nuanced with baptismal and marital overtones: "My hand was given to Christ, who led me into the water and stripped me of my clothing, which at once vanished from sight. Christ then appeared to wash me, the water feeling quite warm." She goes on to say that during this time there was a "profound silence" from the shore. When she emerged from the water an angel provided a clean, white robe that the Father put on her. Then she heard incredible music and shouting. As they all went back to the tree where she had first encountered the Trinity, the Holy Spirit plucked some fruit from the tree and gave it to Foote. After she had eaten it, God the Father told her she was now ready to be sent into the world to go where he would command.[13]

In response to her questions about what to do if she was not accepted or believed (she was, after all, a woman, African-American, and poor), Jesus wrote golden words with golden ink and placed the scroll containing the words in her bosom. He said she could show them to the people and they would believe. The vision ended as she was led with a singing throng to a beautiful gate.[14]

13. Foote, "A Brand Plucked from the Fire," 202–3.
14. Ibid., 203.

The vision had lasted through the night, with her behavior strange enough to keep friends and husband at her side.[15] A physician was called but could do nothing to help her. As she awakened from the vision she tried to explain to those around her what had happened. The experience of the scroll was so real that she tried to take it out of her blouse to show her friends, who finally convinced her that it was "in her heart" and would be shown in her life.[16] While her friends were supportive, her minister, Jehiel C. Beman, was not. He listened to her story with contempt and disbelief, the beginning of what became Foote's eventual excommunication from the AME Zion Church. Her husband had already turned against her holiness spirituality.[17]

A Voice for Equality in Christ

From the day of her call Foote experienced both fruitfulness in her evangelistic ministry and ongoing persecution and suffering at the hands of Christians. When she went to her AME Zion Conference to protest the excommunication, which was based on her gender, spirituality, and call to preach, she was brushed off, her letter of petition thrown under a table. Describing the event, Foote wrote, "there was no justice meted out to women in those days. Even ministers of Christ did not feel that women had any rights which they were bound to respect."[18] Thus Foote saw the political and ecclesiastical oppression of women as the misuse of power and an injustice in both realms. As William Andrews notes, Foote's choice of language in this statement is a parody of Chief Justice Roger B. Taney in the

15. It is not clear from the text exactly what her external behavior was during the vision.

16. Foote, "A Brand Plucked from the Fire," 203.

17. Julia describes how even prior to her call to preach her husband gradually resisted her holiness spirituality and began to verbally abuse her, telling her that he was going to send her to the "crazy house." She said that from that time forward there was "something high and dark," a spiritual shadow that remained between her husband and herself. He also took a job that kept him at sea for months at a time, leaving Julia lonely and with a sense of vulnerability. Later, God gave to her the promise of Isa. 54:5, that he would be Julia's husband (ibid., 194–96).

18. Ibid., 207.

infamous Dred Scott decision of 1857, in which Taney said that African-Americans "had no rights which the white man was bound to respect."[19]

Foote spent the rest of her life preaching, praying, and teaching the good news of salvation through Jesus Christ. She had a particular charism for leading people out of spiritual bondage into freedom.[20] As was the case with her contemporaries Zilpha Elaw and Jarena Lee, Foote experienced sanctification as a deep reorientation of life away from fear and diminishment, toward boldness, belief in the power and authority of Christ within her, and a willingness to defy social institutions and conventions that were sinful.[21] Holiness, Foote believed, included a radical and liberating call to equality between women and men, between black and white. Galatians 3:28 and numerous other texts were cited to provide her apologetic for women's preaching and for the equality of women and men. In regard to racism and classism, Foote criticized the white church for being "deluded by a spirit of error, which leads them to say to the poor and the colored ones among them, 'Stand back a little—I am holier than thou.'"[22] She described the experience of African-American Christians in the white church as being treated like lepers, people who are ritually and permanently unclean.[23]

Like Phoebe Palmer, Foote's authority to critique the church (along with her authority to preach the gospel in general) was based primarily on God's word. As one who had to be convinced by the Triune God that she had indeed been called to a ministry that she had previously believed was barred to women, Foote searched the Scriptures, finding ample precedent for her prophetic calling both in the Old and New Testaments.

19. Andrews, ed., *Sisters in the Spirit*, 20.

20. Ibid., 16.

21. Ibid.

22. Ibid., 167. In these ways Foote was a protowomanist with her integrated analysis and critique of racism, sexism, and classism in the church. See Emilie M. Townes, ed., *A Troubling in My Soul: Womanist Perspectives on Evil and Suffering* (Maryknoll, NY: Orbis, 1993), 2.

23. This comment is included in Foote's description of her parents' conversion and their cold reception in the local Methodist Episcopal Church (Foote, "A Brand Plucked from the Fire," 167).

Foote's primary phrase to describe herself was "a brand plucked from the burning," referencing the vision of Zechariah 3:2.[24] In this phrase it is striking that she identifies with Joshua, the high priest who is accused by Satan but beloved and called by God. Joshua appears before God in filthy clothes, stained not by his own sin but by the trial of being plucked from Jerusalem, which is burning in judgment. God gives Joshua clean garments and a new turban that represent his new, priestly mission. Foote's sacred reading of her own life, conversion, and call, the "re-storying of her life"[25] along the lines of the Zechariah text, was extraordinary in its empowerment of her to be able to withstand persecution, hardship, and illness as she faithfully carried out her evangelistic ministry. She was indeed, through her excommunication, hurled out from a church in need of judgment, because of its sexism, racism, and classism, to evangelize all who would receive her. Throughout her ministry, this "brand plucked from the burning" was very clear that until the sins of race, gender, and class were no longer part of the ecclesiastical system, the church was deluded. Until the church stopped treating its own members as "lepers," ritually and permanently unclean because of race, gender, or class, it was disobedient to the will of God and, in fact, in collusion with Satan, the Accuser.

The Church Deluded Today

It has been more than a century since Foote preached her last sermon. Though some progress has been made toward racial and gender equality in some segments of the church, for the most part the church continues to be riddled with the unholy syncretism of Christianity and patriarchy, racism, and classism. This is true whether the church is African-American, Asian, Latino, or Caucasian.[26] It is true in virtually

24. Ibid., 168, 178, 181, 189, 191.
25. Conversion as the re-storying of one's life in the stories of the Bible is a favorite theme of Brueggemann and Brad J. Kallenberg. See Walter Brueggemann, *Biblical Perspectives on Evangelism* (Nashville: Abingdon, 1993); and Brad J. Kallenberg, *Live to Tell: Evangelism in a Postmodern Age* (Grand Rapids: Brazos, 2002).
26. In citing these four categories, I am not offering an essentialist or simplistic analysis of the church in terms of race and class. As Kwok Pui-lan demonstrates in *Postcolonial Imagination and Feminist Theology* (Louisville: Westminster John Knox, 2005), the designation of African-American, Asian, Latino, and Caucasian are not

all denominations. It is true in mainline denominations such as the United Methodist Church, in which women are ordained but are paid less than men and receive a disproportionate number of appointments to small, declining, and dysfunctional churches.[27] It is true in urban African-American churches surrounded by Latino neighbors but with none of them in the church. It is true in Asian churches where women remain subservient and ethnicity takes priority over the gospel.

In many ways the evangelical Protestant church has moved backward in the past hundred years. Early in the twentieth century evangelicals in the holiness movement were at the forefront of the women's rights movement in the United States.[28] At that time a number of evangelical denominations ordained women—denominations that today either do not ordain women or make it very hard for women who are called to remain in their evangelical contexts.[29] In the 1920s, for example, the Reverend Dr. John Roach Straton, a prominent leader of the fundamentalist movement and pastor of Calvary Baptist Church in New York City, was a staunch supporter of Uldine Utley

---

four monolithic categories, but four rubrics under which there are myriad variations of cultures, experiences, and theological perspectives. For example, even a small Caucasian congregation in Youngstown, Ohio, may include persons from several distinctly different cultures, including steel mill workers, recovering drug addicts, public school teachers, and a lawyer or two. This little church is multicultural and not simply a "white church." Even so, it is important for the purposes of our current discussion to note in more general terms that the three-headed monster of sexism, racism, and classism is found almost universally in the church.

27. At this time only 13 percent of United Methodist elders are women, and women make up only 2 percent of United Methodist senior pastors of churches with memberships larger than one thousand. While 35 percent of elders under the age of thirty-five are women, reflecting a shift toward more women in ordained ministry in the UMC, the actual percentage of elders (male or female) under the age of thirty-five has fallen drastically in the last twenty years, making this figure less than promising. See www.gcsrw.org/research/index.htm; www.gcsrw.org/newsarchives/2006/060319 .htm; and Lovett H. Weems Jr., "Leadership for Reaching Emerging Generations." *Circuit Rider* (March–April 2006): 4–7.

28. See Janette Hassey, *No Time for Silence: Evangelical Women in Public Ministry around the Turn of the Century* (Grand Rapids: Academie, 1986), 123–43.

29. For detailed studies of the pressures against evangelical women as leaders in evangelical institutions, see Christine Pohl and Nicola Hoggard Creegan, *Living on the Boundaries: Evangelical Women, Feminism and the Theological Academy* (Downers Grove, IL: InterVarsity, 2006); and Julie Ingersoll, *Evangelical Christian Women: War Stories in the Gender Battles* (New York: New York University Press, 2003).

and her right to preach. He defended Utley's call using Scripture.[30] Utley's freedom to follow her call would be repressed in the same tradition today.

In many evangelical churches women's ordination and the equality of women and men are presented pejoratively, as examples of the church sinfully accommodating the "Godless, secular feminist movement" of the late twentieth century, with its alleged desire to destroy family values and remove all distinctions between women and men.[31] Far from the truth, these allegations ignore the reality that the vision of equality emerges from the Bible itself, and from the call to evangelism given to marginalized people by the Triune God. It is a vision with a very long history of repression.

The nineteenth-century impetus for the right of women to preach and other women's rights came in large part from holiness pneumatology, such as that of Phoebe Palmer and Julia Foote. The argument for gender and racial equality came from a careful reading and critical exegesis of Scripture. Since the Holy Spirit had been given to all people, with Acts 2 describing sons and daughters, old and young alike receiving gifts for public ministry, all people were equally worthy in the eyes of God. The Holy Spirit, not men and not religious institutions, determines the distribution of spiritual gifts.[32] As found in the title of Phoebe Palmer's landmark book, this equal call and empowerment for mission was "the promise of the Father" for all future generations. While there were social and political ramifications to their emphasis on racial and gender equality, for these early holiness pioneers the driving concern was obedience to God's call to evangelistic mission.

Such a call was healing and liberating for women who had been indoctrinated to accept patriarchy and its ensuing, multiple forms of violence as "just the way things are," or even as the way God intended. For African-American women in particular, the Jesus of

---

30. Priscilla Pope-Levison, *Turn the Pulpit Loose: Two Centuries of American Women Evangelists* (New York: Palgrave MacMillan, 2004), 230.

31. Those who signed the Danvers Statement are representative of this position. For more information on the group that advocates this position, The Council on Biblical Manhood and Womanhood, and the Danver's statement itself, see www.cbmw.org/Resources/Articles/The-Danvers-Statement.

32. 1 Cor. 12:11.

Julia Foote was the healer of the wounds received from racist and patriarchal institutions.[33] This is seen in the vision in which Foote received her call to ministry, in the removal of her tattered garments, and in Jesus's gentle washing of her body. Through Jesus's sanctifying touch her femaleness, her physical body, mind, spirit, and vocation were all declared good and holy. She experienced a transformed vision of herself as a woman, an African-American, and a preacher. Foote's vision contains many elements of healing and empowerment that are found in the experiences of other women mystics, both her contemporaries and those of earlier days. Just as Foote was initially apprehensive about God's wrath and damnation toward her, only to be surprised with the kindness of Jesus, Foote's contemporaries Zilpha Elaw and Jarena Lee both had conversion experiences in which they were anxious and conscious of sin but saw Christ and God smiling at them. For all three women Christ offered salvation through hospitable, healing images.[34] All three learned to ignore "the evil voice of discouragement" and to "trust in the godly voice of affirmation and empowerment as authoritative," for their intimacy with God in prayer and mystical experiences taught them to trust the love of God.[35]

It is clear from Foote's ministry that she did not simply appropriate these themes of empowerment, healing, liberation, and a new identity for herself alone. Grounded in her biblical pneumatology and Christology, mystically experienced in her life of prayer, Foote's message

33. Womanist views of Jesus's healing of women suffering from racist and sexist sin are most creatively expressed through sermons and novels written by African-American women, including Alice Walker and Toni Morrison. Though treating theodicy in the context of a racist, sexist culture, these texts usually are not included in the official canon of systematic theology in its discussion of theodicy, because they are from suppressed voices and because of their "non-academic" genres (Katie Geneva Cannon, "The Wounds of Jesus: Justification of Goodness in the Face of Manifold Evil," in Townes, ed., A Troubling in My Soul, 219–31).

34. Karen Baker-Fletcher, "Voice, Vision, and Spirit: Black Preaching Women in Nineteenth Century America," in Sisters Struggling in the Spirit: A Women of Color Theological Anthology, ed. Nantawan Boonprasat Lewis (Louisville: Women's Ministries Program Area National Ministries Division, Presbyterian Church [USA], 1994), 36. All three women also experienced visions, voices, and other kataphatic phenomena when they were called into evangelistic ministry (ibid., 39).

35. Ibid., 41.

of good news was one of liberation and healing for all people. It was prophetic not only toward a sexist, racist, classist world but especially toward the church that was "deluded" by a "spirit of error."

Mechthild of Magdeburg and the Beguines

Hundreds of years before Julia Foote was "a brand plucked from the burning," a movement arose among lay women for whom the call to apostolic mission proved irresistible. They were the Beguines, a diverse group of women who gathered to live an unofficial monastic life in small groups of varying sizes. Their purpose was to be an alternative vision of Christian community in the midst of a church suffering from the same misogyny, materialism, and abuse of power Foote would name centuries later.[36]

The original Beguines, contemporaries of the early Dominicans and Franciscans, were found in the German lowlands.[37] They were contemplatives, mystics, and healers. Their healing ministry was expressed in three ways: living in self-supporting community, grounding their lives in contemplative prayer, and caring for the poor and sick. In a way they were the original Missionaries of Charity,[38] especially

36. Saskia Murk-Jansen, *Brides in the Desert: The Spirituality of the Beguines* (Maryknoll, NY: Orbis, 1998), 15.

37. For a detailed recent study of the early Beguines see Walter Simons, *Cities of Ladies: Beguine Communities in the Medieval Low Countries, 1200–1565* (Philadelphia: University of Pennsylvania Press, 2001). Especially interesting is Simons's discussion of the etymology of the name "Beguine." Though the origins of the name have long been disputed, Simons argues persuasively for its similarity to the name "Lollards," meaning "mumblers," referring to the practice of barely audible praying or singing. The name was pejorative, mocking the Beguines for their language of prayer (ibid., 121–23).

38. The Missionaries of Charity is an order that was founded in 1950 by Mother Teresa (Agnes Gonxa Bojaxhiu), winner of the 1979 Nobel Peace Prize for her work among the poor in Calcutta. For more on Mother Teresa, see Mother Teresa, *In My Own Words*, comp. José Luis Gonzáles-Balado (New York: Gramercy, 1997); John J. Kirvan, *Love without Measure: The Spirituality of Service of Mother Teresa* (Notre Dame, IN: Ave Maria Press, 2004); and David Scott, *A Revolution of Love: The Meaning of Mother Teresa* (Chicago: Loyola Press, 2005). The most recent book about Mother Teresa that has rocked the world with its description of her long experience of the dark night of the soul is *Come Be My Light* by Mother Teresa and Brian Kolodiejchuk (New York: Doubleday, 2007).

noted for their work among lepers.[39] Like Mother Teresa, the Beguines believed that God is found among the poor and despised of
the world. Their goal was to know experientially the "otherness" of
God's kenotic love. The Beguines' contemplative spirituality was the
source of their vision, strength, power, and endurance, even to the
point of martyrdom.

Beguines carried out their ministry without the formal sanction
of the church, one of the biggest reasons they were later persecuted
by the church.[40] They embraced the monastic disciplines of poverty,
chastity, and service to God, with each group having its own spiritual
practices and forms of service.[41] Rather than impacting the world
through teaching or preaching, as did the Franciscans and Dominicans, the Beguines' ethos was one of embodied holiness of heart
and life. In the beginning people marveled at the purity of heart, the
holy simplicity, and the apostolic power of their lives. They initially
received appreciative comments, even from Pope Honarius III and Pope
Gregory IX.[42] But the glad reception of their ministry was short-lived
due to the reactions of certain clerics who resented their independent
spirit and influence among the laity and many religious, especially
the Dominicans. William of St. Amour led the persecution of the
Beguines that became so severe that within a hundred years of their
inception they were nearly wiped out.[43] His aversion for the Beguines
was focused on one woman in particular, a mystic named Mechthild of

39. Murk-Jansen, *Brides in the Desert*, 11.

40. Beguines still exist today in and beyond the southern Low Countries of Western Europe. Their origins, however, rest in a period of history in which numerous
monastic reform movements erupted, including the Dominicans and Franciscans. The
Beguine movement was one of those movements: Spirit-led forms of authentic faith
and community that were nonschismatic yet prophetic during a time of corruption
and materialism in the church (Simons, *Cities of Ladies*, ix). Beghards were the male
counterparts of the Beguines and lived in similar communities, but for the purposes
of this chapter our focus is on the Beguines.

41. One cannot speak of "Beguine spirituality" as a monolithic reality, in other
words. There were varieties of Beguine spiritualities. What was common to all of
them was the desire to live an apostolic life in community and to do so without an
official mandate from the church.

42. Frank Tobin, introduction to *The Flowing Light of the Godhead*, by Mechthild
of Magdeburg, Classics of Western Spirituality, trans. Frank Tobin, preface by Margot
Schmidt (New York: Paulist Press, 1998), 2.

43. Murk-Jansen, *Brides in the Desert*, 29–30.

Magdeburg (1208–1282/94). Despite his efforts to destroy Mechthild and her book, Mechthild lived into old age, and her *Flowing Light of the Godhead* was one of the mystical texts of the Beguines that survived the persecution.[44]

Like Foote and many other women mystics, Mechthild faced much opposition and persecution, partly because of her gender and partly because of her power. No small part of her sufferings came because of her prophetic critique of the religious leaders of her day for their lack of holiness and their hostility toward passionate spirituality. These same kinds of criticisms were characteristic of Foote and other nineteenth-century holiness leaders who called the church to renewal. Mechthild's work offers many insights for today's church, but of special interest are two themes that parallel Foote's central concerns: the love of God for the "least of these" and the blight of self-serving, unjust clergy.

From the age of twelve Mechthild experienced what she called "greetings" from the Holy Spirit.[45] These were kataphatic encounters with the love of God that happened daily for thirty-one years. Using the language of courtly love, Mechthild writes sensually of the passionate love between God and the human soul. For example, in "God Caresses the Soul in Six Ways" she draws from the erotic imagery of the Song of Songs, giving voice to God's delight in the human soul who will receive him:

> You are my softest pillow,
> My most lovely bed,
> My most intimate repose,
> My deepest longing,
> My most sublime glory.
> You are an allurement to my Godhead.

44. The Beguines were among the first to write theological work in the vernacular (Low Middle German), thus subverting the control of religious texts by the church hierarchy. Their status as lay women made their bold move even more offensive as time passed and as they gained increasing influence with their theology and ministry. Marguerite of Poirete, a Beguine, was burned at the stake for her book, *A Mirror of Simple Souls*, in June 1310 (Murk-Jansen, *Brides of the Desert*, 29–30). *Flowing Light of the Godhead* is no longer extant in its original language, and the first English edition, translated by Frank Tobin, was published in 1998.

45. Mechthild, *Flowing Light of the Godhead*, 139.

A thirst for my humanity,
A stream for my burning.[46]

While her book includes references to her own mystical visions and experiences, the primary theme is the depth of God's love for humanity. Along with other Beguine mystics, Mechthild sees this love as terrible in its willingness to suffer and give, a kind of love that caused Christ to want to die and descend to hell for his beloved. As Mechthild grew older, she began to undergo a dark night of the soul that grew deeper as the years went by. Though painful and difficult, Mechthild embraced the apophatic way, for she believed that God is never closer than in the longing emptiness of the night. Her description of her dark night in many ways foreshadows that of John of the Cross, whose work would come some three hundred years later.[47] Mechthild's seven books were written during a period of many years and gathered into one volume, *Flowing Light of the Godhead*. Although her lyrical prose, prayers, and poetry of the first three books do communicate the passionate, kataphatic experiences she had, Mechthild is ever drawn downward toward kenosis and has much to say about union with Christ in suffering. Her scathing critique of self-centered clergy is woven through her discussions of the sufferings of Christ with his people, for these clergy are the source of much of the suffering. The final books are the darkest, focusing on the apophatic union of God and the human soul.

Though Mechthild did not address racism as such, gender and poverty played a significant role in her Christology. She saw herself and other women being especially chosen as messengers to the church as an expression of kenosis on the part of God. In other words, the nature of divine love is to go as low as possible to serve the beloved. God tells Mechthild that "the course of my Holy Spirit flows by nature down hill."[48] As Mechthild understood it, God could go no lower in

---

46. Ibid., 48.
47. Schmidt, preface to Mechthild, *Flowing Light of the Godhead*.
48. Mechthild, *Flowing Light of the Godhead*, 97. Interestingly, Hannah Hurnard offers a similar position in the Water Song in her allegory *Hinds Feet on High Places* ([Wheaton: Tyndale, 1986], 185), in which the water sings that its greatest joy is to "answer the call" to flow down "to the lowest place of all." Like Mechthild's theology, Hurnard's allegory and imagery draw heavily from the Song of Songs.

a patriarchal world[49] than to come in the form of simple, poor, often uneducated lay women and speak through them to the church and the world.[50] Among the most grievous offenses she named against the clergy was their failure to understand this obvious truth. When they rejected her writing and her ministry because of her gender, they were rejecting Christ in his kenotic love.

Just as Foote warns that anyone who scoffs at her book would do so at the peril of his soul,[51] Mechthild explains that God assuages her fear that her book will be burned, reminding her that anyone who tries to destroy her book will have to take it from God's own hand.[52] Brother Heinrich, the Dominican who wrote the preface to Mechthild's original book, declares that the real author of the book was the Father, Son, and Holy Spirit.[53] He offers a brief but pointed apologetic for Mechthild's ministry, arguing from the holiness of Mechthild's life and citing Deborah and Hulda as biblical examples of women whom God had called to prophetic ministry explicitly for the liberation of God's people.[54] Thus Mechthild's advocate and friend, Brother Heinrich, clearly saw Mechthild's message as one for the church in bondage, or as Foote would say, "deluded by a spirit of error." The delusion had much to do with its subjugation and silencing of women.

Just as Foote likened herself to Joshua the high priest (a brand plucked from the burning), Mechthild locates her life in the life of Christ, as she is called on to "drain many a chalice of gall because, alas, the devil still has many a one among religious people willing to pour it out."[55] Such suffering at the hands of the church, she emphasizes, is a necessary part of union with Christ. Like many other Beguines, Mechthild sees the kataphatic ecstasies of mystical union

49. Of course, Mechthild did not use the word "patriarchal," but the problem of patriarchy is clearly evident in her critique of the clergy.

50. Rosemary Radford Ruether, *Visionary Women: Three Medieval Mystics* (Minneapolis: Augsburg Fortress, 2002), 32.

51. Foote, "A Brand Plucked from the Fire," 226.

52. Mechthild, *Flowing Light of the Godhead*, 96.

53. Ibid., 32. Again, Heinrich's language is simply an affirmation that Mechthild's inspiration for the book was the Triune God.

54. Ibid., 31–32.

55. Ibid., 90–91.

as something found early in the spiritual journey. Deeper union with Christ involves kenosis, the suffering of the cross as one gives oneself in service. With graphically descriptive language, Mechthild gives voice to Christ calling his church to sacrificial love, to be companions with him through "twenty-three steps of the cross."[56] The steps enumerate the many forms of betrayal, abuse, loss, grief, false accusations, beatings, torture, and, finally, the death of Christ. The final steps, however, are those of resurrection and victory, offering those who travel the way of the cross hope for redemption and ultimate healing of all wounds.

Confessing the Threefold Sin, Healing the Threefold Wound

There is no greater challenge to the church in the night than to relinquish its idolatrous and syncretistic attachment to sexism, racism, and classism, for this trio of evil ideologies has been embedded in the American church from the time Christianity made its way across the Atlantic with the first explorers. The history of the church in America is, along with other stories, a long story of church-sanctioned injustice as women and ethnic minorities have been forced to live their faith from the margins. It is a story of Christians owning, raping, and whipping slaves, of using black women as breeders to expand the slave industry. It is a story of the genocide of countless Native Americans in the name of manifest destiny. It is a story of denominations forming explicitly to serve one race while excluding others, and of congregations moving from their "changing" neighborhood to the suburbs so they don't have to be in fellowship with "those people."

It is a story of how the church has lost credibility in a secular culture in which women and people of diverse ethnicity are senators, physicians, lawyers, and professors, but in the church are segregated, silenced, excluded, and invisible. It is a story of seminaries splitting over the right of women to be ordained. It is a story of battered women being told by pastors to go home and submit to their violent husbands so as to win them in meekness and silence. It is a story of a democratic nation in which poverty forces more than forty-five

56. Ibid., 54.

million Americans to forego adequate health care because they cannot afford health insurance,[57] while churches build sprawling campuses that resemble palatial resorts. It is the story of a church deluded by a spirit of error.

The church in the night is being called to own and renounce its threefold syncretistic attachment to sexism, racism, and classism. These attachments have wounded the church and have caused the church to wound the world for far too long. Painful self-reflection, repentance, and much theological work are needed to retrieve the egalitarian ethos of the gospel. As the church is healed from this damaging threefold wound, it will regain the moral authority it needs to speak to a world hurtling toward chaos. Delivered of its demonic attachment to oppressive power, the church will find its God-given conscience toward all living things that have suffered under the centripetal force of domination. The earth and all its creatures will once again become primary foci of the good news, that God is redeeming not just fallen humans but the whole of creation.[58]

57. The number of Americans unable to afford health care is increasing exponentially. Lack of adequate health care is just one of the many forms of deprivation and poverty experienced by a growing number of working Americans. To better understand the rapidly increasing numbers of the working poor, the depth of their poverty, and their day-to-day realities in America, see Barbara Ehrenreich, *Nickel and Dimed: On (Not) Getting By in America* (New York: Metropolitan/Owl, 2001).

58. Rom. 8:18–22.

6

Redeeming the Earth

Dozens of them were in the darkened rooms, people posed in various activities as if they had been playing freeze tag. Foot thrust upward, a young man kicked a soccer ball. A man was on a rearing horse, someone was lost in thought before a chess table, a man was leaping high in a martial arts move. A woman eight months pregnant was resting on her side, her unborn child visibly curled in repose. Each of their bodies was perfectly preserved, yet they seemed alive, as if they had been caught in action and might at any moment resume what they had been doing. This seemed true despite their being without skin. Along with glass cases of intestines, hearts, livers, lungs, and brains, every major system of the human body had been opened to plain view through a mysterious process called "plastination."[1] What surprised me the most about "Body Worlds," a science exhibit, was

1. The process of plastination was developed by Dr. Gunther von Hagens in 1977. It involves the use of polymer chemistry to preserve the body in lifelike appearance. The people had donated their bodies while they were alive, giving themselves to an unprecedented project in the field of anatomy (www.bodyworlds.com/en/plastination/plastination_process.html).

the effect it had on its audience.[2] Scores of silent people made their way through, gazing in mute wonder. Some wiped tears from their eyes. The science of anatomy had been swallowed in mystery. It was a spiritual experience. This happened without words, without doctrines, without religious statements. An encounter with the Creator took place in an encounter with creation.

What people experienced at Body Worlds is a microcosm of what God intends for the world at large. Everything about God's creation is meant to tell us something about God. Creation is meant to lead us to worship. Yet the material world in which we live—the water, air, and soil, the ecosystems—faces perils unimagined even a hundred years ago. We hurtle toward landscapes that used to belong to science fiction.

Borne along on a mechanistic worldview, driven by greed, the commodification of science and technology is unleashing one hell after another on the world. The rocks cry out through strip mines and the rubble of Iraq. The forests cry out as 150,000 square kilometers are permanently destroyed every year.[3] Fish and birds cry out as they swallow pesticides and suffocate in oil spills. The children cry out, thirty thousand every day as they die from lack of food and water.[4] Creation groans, Paul writes, waiting for redemption to come through the children of God.[5] What the church thinks about creation has never been more important. What the church does about God's creation is a matter of life and death.

As the church in the night responds to a world in trauma it needs the creation theology of two mystics, one a theologian, the other a tailor. Grounded in the witness of Scripture, using the language of their day, St. Bonaventure and John Woolman offer a vision of redemption in which environmental ethics and salvation go hand in hand.[6]

2. Several Body Worlds exhibits have made their way around the world in recent years. My family and I visited the exhibit in Dallas in March 2007 (Institute for Plastination, "Body Worlds: An Anatomical Success Story," www.bodyworlds.com/en/prelude.html).

3. Rainforest Foundation, "The Destruction of Rainforests," www.rainforest foundationuk.org/s-The%20Destruction%20of%20Rainforests.

4. UNICEF, "Facts on Children," www.unicef.org/media/media_9475.html.

5. Rom. 8:19–23.

6. They do not use the modern phrase "environmental ethics," of course, but their theology expresses these commitments.

Every Creature a Divine Word

Bonaventure, christened Giovanni di Fidanza, was born in Bagnoregie in the Papal States in 1217, a contemporary of Thomas Aquinas. When Bonaventure was a child he became gravely ill, prompting his mother to vow that should her son recover she would devote him to Francis of Assisi.[7] After regaining health the young Bonaventure became a steadfast devotee of Francis, entering the Franciscan order in 1243. He was educated at the University of Paris where, like Aquinas, he also taught, and eventually became Cardinal Bishop of Albano, where he served as a frequent adviser to the pope. Centuries later he was canonized and named a doctor of the church.[8] Bonaventure's writing is a unique blend of systematic theology, psychology, and mysticism.[9]

For Bonaventure there is no divide between sacred and secular, material and spiritual. Life points to God. "Every creature, because it speaks God, is a divine word,"[10] Bonaventure writes. Creation is iconic. From seagulls to stars, from a grain of sand to a snow-capped peak, each created thing contains a unique "footprint" of God.[11] The earth and all its creatures are sacred, none of them to be taken for granted, all of them to be treated with respect. Through creation God intends to lead humanity to true worship, with the highest expression of God's self-revelation found when the Word becomes flesh.

The central motif of Bonaventure's complex thought is the concept of *exitus reditus*, meaning that all of creation comes forth from God and returns to God. Creation is the joyous overflow of the relationship of Father, Son, and Holy Spirit, as water bubbles forth from a

7. St. Francis of Assisi (1182–1228) is the patron saint of ecology.

8. Guy J. Bougerol, *Introduction to the Works of Bonaventure* (Paterson, NJ: St. Anthony Guild Press, 1964), 3.

9. Bonaventure's two greatest masterpieces are *Breviloquium*, a seven-part summary of his systematic theology, using the seven days of creation as a metaphoric framework, and *The Soul's Journey into God*, a guide for the systematic, subjective contemplation of God that is developed in seven chapters treating God's self-revelation in Traces, Image, Being, and Mystical Ravishment.

10. Quoted in Dominic Monti, "St. Bonaventure," in *The Harper Collins Encyclopedia of Catholicism*, ed. Richard P. McBrien (San Francisco: HarperSanFrancisco, 1995), 190.

11. Bonaventure, *Breviloquium*, 2.11.2. Citations for this and subsequent references to the *Breviloquium* are from *The Works of Bonaventure*, vol. 2, *The Breviloquium*, trans. José de Vinck (Paterson, NJ: St. Anthony Guild Press, 1963).

fountain. Originating as an idea of the Father, each created thing
mirrors some aspect of Christ, and through the Holy Spirit returns
to God in consummation as it fulfills its intended creaturely purpose.
In this way every created thing participates in or "recapitulates" the
jubilant inner life of the Trinity.[12] When all of creation is unhindered
in recapitulating the Trinity, all of creation is brought into harmony,
experiencing mystical unity amid diversity.[13] To put it in contemporary
terms, when creatures and ecosystems function in healthy interde-
pendence, the dynamic life of God is revealed. When creatures and
ecosystems are hindered or oppressed, that life is obscured.

Bonaventure sometimes calls Christ the Divine Art, for creation is
patterned after Christ and was made by Christ. Christ is both Exemplar for creation and the image of the unseen God. Christ is the sum
of all perfections in the universe. Bonaventure asserts that the incarnation of Christ was not brought about by sin. Rather, the incarnation
is the final perfection of creation, the completion of the universe. "As
the most noble of God's works, the Incarnation is willed for its own
sake, and not for the sake of any lesser good."[14] Since all of creation
mirrors Christ, creation is therefore made in the image of God.

Does this mean that humans are not uniquely created in the image
of God? Not at all. For Bonaventure humanity offers a fuller recapitulation of God than the "lower" forms of creation.[15] This is true because
all lower forms are contained within humanity on some elemental
level. That is, water, air, plant life, the basic elements all are contained
within humans. To use the language of Genesis 2:7, humanity is made

12. Leonard Bowman argues that while Bonaventure does not use the term "recapitulation," preferring "participation," his meaning is more adequately expressed in
contemporary meanings of "recapitulation" (Leonard J. Bowman, "Cosmic Exemplarism of Bonaventure," *Journal of Religion* [April 1975]: 185).

13. Ibid., 184–85.

14. Zachary Hayes, "Incarnation and Creation in the Theology of St. Bonaventure," in *Studies Honoring Ignatius Charles Brady, Friar Minor*, ed. Romano Stephen
Almagno and Conrad L. Harkins (St. Bonaventure, NY: Franciscan Institute, 1976),
328.

15. Like his contemporaries, Bonaventure accepted a hierarchy of creation, but in
his understanding of exemplarity he differed from the standard view. Every created
thing is equally close to Christ the Exemplar, so there is no diminished significance
to creatures that are lower in the hierarchy. This belief implies an inherent respect
for the "lower" creatures.

of "clay." In this sense there is a unique "fullness" to the creatures called humans. Yet there is more. Humanity is both clay and divine breath, made of a composite of body and soul, so that not only does humanity contain within itself all "lower" forms of creation, but in Christ humanity also becomes mediator for the return of all things to the Creator. Humanity bears a unique responsibility to facilitate the healing of creation.

Finally, because humans are capable of receiving God's self-revelation, they have the fullest potential to image God to the rest of creation. In Bonaventure's doctrine of *imago Dei*, humanity is uniquely charged to image the second person of the Trinity, in that humans should mirror God as Jesus mirrors God, as beloved children of God.[16] Creation should see in redeemed humanity the same loving care and respect that God has for his creation.

Bonaventure describes two books of revelation through which humanity comes to know God: the book of creation and the book of Scripture.[17] For Bonaventure, creation alone was originally an adequate revelation of God to humanity, but since the fall people are like illiterates trying in vain to read the book of creation.[18] For that reason they need the Bible through which to interpret the world.[19] Unless the soul is cleansed and submitted to God, efforts to understand the two books are fruitless.[20] Through a work of grace called "contuition" the mirror of the soul is "cleansed and polished" by God. It then becomes able to understand the books and reflect God to the world.

In Bonaventure's mind the goal of contemplating God through creation is holiness, union with God. Significantly, Bonaventure sees the final stages of contemplation as a movement away from kataphatic

16. Hayes, "Incarnation and Creation," 318.

17. Bonaventure, *Breviloquium*, 2.5.1, 2.

18. Ibid., 2.12.4, 5. Here he sounds very much like Julian of Norwich in the Servant Parable, in which blindness and intellectual darkness are characteristics of the fallen servant.

19. As Bowman explains, for Bonaventure creation may be read with the four "senses" of medieval exegesis: literal, allegorical, tropological, and anagogical (Bowman, "Cosmic Exemplarism," 185).

20. Bonaventure, *The Soul's Journey into God, The Tree of Life, The Life of St. Francis*, Classics of Western Spirituality, trans. and with an introduction by Ewert Cousins (New York: Paulist Press, 1978), 56.

reflection on creation, toward apophatic contemplation of the Trinity, since God is uncreated.[21] Thus while Bonaventure presents a vision of the immanence of God in creation, he begins and ends with Christ the Triune Creator. Christ is the Alpha and Omega. Laying the foundation of an interdependent, redemptive relationship between humans and the rest of creation, Bonaventure's vision of salvation flows from Christ through the church, out into the world.

The Gospel of Enough

Like Bonaventure, John Woolman envisioned the holy life as the exercise of justice and peace not only among people, but between people, animals, and the rest of creation. The same sense of justice that drove Woolman's resistance to slavery fueled his commitment to the well-being of animals and the earth. For Woolman "true religion" consisted of an inward life of devotion expressed in an outward life of goodness to all living things. In today's language, Woolman would be called a Christian conservationist and human rights activist.

Woolman (1720–1772) grew up in a devout Quaker family, the fourth of thirteen children.[22] His father was a farmer who encouraged Woolman toward the contemplative life. He left his parents' farm at age twenty-one to take a job in a retail shop in the small town of Mt. Holly, not far from Philadelphia. Some time later Woolman went into retail business for himself, quite successfully. But it wasn't long before his growing affluence began to trouble the young man. It became increasingly clear to him that the accumulation of wealth by the few required a network of oppressive systems built on the exploitation of people, animals, and the land. He could no longer in good conscience pursue what is today called the American dream.

21. Bonaventure, *Soul's Journey into God,* 114.
22. This biographic sketch draws from Phillips P. Moulton, introduction to *The Journal and Major Essays of John Woolman,* by John Woolman, ed. Phillips P. Moulton (Richmond, IN: Friends United Press, 1989), 3–16; David Morse, *Testimony: John Woolman on Today's Global Economy* (Wallingford, PA: Pendle Hill Publications, 2001); and Frederick B. Tolles, introduction to *The Journal of John Woolman and a Plea for the Poor,* by John Woolman, ed. Frederick B. Tolles (New York: Corinth Books, 1961), v–xii.

Eventually Woolman left the retail business and became a tailor so he could more easily limit his work to a level of adequacy in supporting himself and his family. In addition to tailoring Woolman kept an orchard, prepared legal documents for people, and did some teaching.[23] He was recorded as an itinerant Quaker minister at the age of twenty-three, meaning his local congregation recognized in him special preaching gifts, issuing a certificate to affirm his call.

By the time Woolman died of smallpox at age fifty-two, he had made about thirty missionary journeys throughout the New England colonies and the Carolinas. His wife, Sarah, and their daughter, Mary, stayed at home when he traveled.[24] Woolman urged the abolition of slavery, the cultivation of a life of simplicity, respect and care for creation, and the end to unjust systems of labor that created poverty and oppression. His preferred method of confrontation with slaveholders and other perpetrators of injustice was individual conversation.[25] His manner of speaking to people was humble and kind, even when confronting them for evil deeds. Most of his journal was written during his missionary travels, after age thirty-six.

Woolman describes early in his journal his first awareness of sins against creation in his memory of having killed a robin and her babies for sport when he was a child. While out playing one day, Woolman had come across a robin sitting on her nest. As she flew around the nest in an effort to protect her young, Woolman used the mother for target practice. Eventually his stone found its mark and the robin fell dead. Though at first he was pleased with himself, Woolman was soon conscience-stricken. He thought about the suffering that the young birds would now experience without their mother to protect and feed them. Woolman decided to be "merciful" and kill the babies too. Afterward the text of Proverbs 12:10, "The mercy of the wicked is cruel," haunted him.[26]

This experience, perhaps, was the beginning of Woolman's lifelong advocacy for animal rights. Throughout his journal and essays, Woolman offers reflections on the vulnerability of animals, their importance to God, and their exploitation and abuse at the hands of humans.

23. Moulton, introduction to *Journals and Major Essays*, 4.
24. Their other daughter died in infancy.
25. Morse, *Testimony*, 5.
26. Moulton, introduction to *Journals and Major Essays*, 24.

Animals and humans exist through the same God-breathed "flame of life," Woolman writes, thus any cruelty displayed against sentient creatures is a contradiction of the love of God.[27] Woolman laments the mistreatment of horses driven to blindness and death through relentless work and whippings, oxen laboring to pull overloaded carts, and insufficient shelter for beasts of burden.[28] True virtue, he writes, necessitates the care of brute beasts as well as people.[29]

Woolman's greatest insights, however, are his connections between the exploitation and abuse of people, animals, and the earth's resources, and systems of political and economic oppression. In his essay "A Plea for the Poor," Woolman describes the multiple layers of oppression involved in the accumulation of wealth. "Every degree of luxury of what kind soever and every demand for money inconsistent with divine order hath some connection with unnecessary labor," he writes.[30] Excess wealth leads to power, Woolman says, which tends to lead to the abuse of power, which ultimately leads to war.[31]

The Christian's vocation, according to Woolman, is to liberate people, animals, and the earth from oppression in whatever form it presents itself. "To labour for a perfect redemption from this spirit of oppression is the greatest business of the whole family of Christ Jesus in this world."[32] But to bring about such liberation, Christians must own their complicity in evil systems, a truth brought home to Woolman through a mystical experience. During a severe illness Woolman experienced a vision in which he saw slaves working in a mine. In the vision the slaves cursed Christ because Christians were the ones who oppressed them, benefiting from their labor and using treasures they produced from the mine. If Christians were this oppressive, the slaves reasoned, Christ must be a "cruel tyrant" indeed. Meanwhile Woolman heard the voice of an angel declaring that he, Woolman, was dead. When he emerged from the vision, Woolman saw silver dishes on the table and realized that the silver had come

27. Ibid., 28.
28. Woolman, *Journal and Major Essays*, 183, 238–39.
29. Ibid., 44.
30. Ibid., 246.
31. Ibid., 255.
32. Ibid., 262.

from slave labor. He understood that the angel's message meant that he was dead to his own will. God was calling him to greater fidelity as a Christian. From that time forward he refused to eat from silver dishes and on numerous occasions used this analogy of silver table services as a means to teach others about injustice.[33] Woolman stopped wearing clothes made with dyed fabric for similar reasons. Throughout his ministry he urged Christians to take note of the hidden costs of luxury, paid for not by the wealthy but by slaves and the poor who labor too hard to provide trinkets for the rich.[34]

Woolman recorded many dreams and visions that shaped his spirituality, but most of his impetus for activism came from living in a culture riddled with injustice. Slavery and the theft of land from Native Americans appalled Woolman, who worked tirelessly to advance abolition. He was among the first proponents of material restitution to slaves and their offspring for having their labor stolen.[35] In the earthy language of a farmer, Woolman says, "To labour too hard or cause others to do so, that we may live conformable to customs which Christ our Redeemer contradicted by his example in the days of his flesh, and which are contrary to divine order, is to manure a soil for the propagating an evil seed in the earth."[36]

The primary business of Christians, according to Woolman, is to "turn all the treasures we possess into the channel of universal love." Since the Creator's will is to watch over all creation with love and mercy, the more holy one becomes, the more one will exercise the gracious love of God for creation. Woolman uses the language of stewardship, explaining that every Christian has gifts from God, and every gift is to be used to bless others. To use our gifts selfishly "disunites" us from God and makes us unworthy stewards.[37]

Woolman notes, however, that to give of ourselves in this way requires an infusion of divine power, because it is beyond human capability to exercise such love.[38] "To labour for an establishment in

33. Ibid., 185–87.
34. Ibid., 244.
35. Ibid., 270–72.
36. Ibid., 247.
37. Ibid., 241, 249.
38. Ibid., 240, 259.

divine love where the mind is disentangled from the power of darkness is the great business of man's life."[39] Left to our own devices, we are sinfully given to hoarding up wealth for ourselves and our descendants. If we used our resources with "pure wisdom" according to the will of God, Woolman writes, there would be enough to go around for everyone. The gospel, when truly lived, is enough.

Eco-evangelism

Deep in the jungles of Thailand in a tiny refugee camp, a man named David Saw Wah is changing the world in a manner that would make Woolman and Bonaventure proud. Wah fled for his life from his home country of Myanmar several years ago. He now lives in a refugee camp, like millions of other people around the world. What makes Wah extraordinary is the way he has transformed the camp into an experiment in sustainable living.[40] Wah plants trees and crops together in small sections of earth, a practice called "agriforestry." He manufactures energy-efficient charcoal briquettes using plant and waste materials from the camp; taps methane gas from pig manure to provide free cooking gas while reducing harmful emissions; purifies water; and in dozens of other ways conserves resources while providing a greatly improved life for his fellow refugees. Wah views his labor as a service not only to those in the camp but also to an endangered planet. Pointing to the charcoal briquettes during an interview with CNN, he noted that they reduce the need to cut down trees. The methane from pig manure contributes less to global warming. Wah hopes for a peaceful future when he and the other refugees can go home, and that when they do they will carry sustainable living with them.

Wah did not talk about religion in his interview with CNN, but his work in the camp is holy. Wah is good news. His edenic transformation of the camp is a picture of what the church is called to do in cities, forests, and deserts around the world. As Bonaventure would put it, every creature is a divine word, a precious resource, and the

---

39. Ibid., 250.

40. Dan Rivers, "Without a Home: Refugees in Crisis," *Anderson Cooper 360*, transcript, http://transcripts.cnn.com/TRANSCRIPTS/0706/20/acd.02.html.

creatures under Wah's care are "unhindered" in the refugee camp. The Trinity dances in the making of briquettes, methane, food, and hope. The glory of God is revealed. Yet this is taking place in a refugee camp, a community made necessary by violence. As long as Christians buy cheap products manufactured by slave labor, we contribute to oppressive political and economic systems that force millions of people, including Wah, into inhumane living conditions, the worst being refugee camps. As Woolman noted, economic injustice can ultimately lead to war, which perpetuates human misery. Until we actively resist the evil of unrestrained consumerism we participate in the sin. Wah's presence in the camp shows us two future paths of eco-evangelism: sustainable living as a central component of stewardship and active resistance to economic, social, and political systems that dehumanize people and degrade God's good earth.

Eco-evangelism, being good news to creation in the name of Jesus, must become key in the mission of the church.[41] As we have seen in the breadth of Bonaventure and Woolman's vision, ecological commitments are not limited to animals, plants, water, and air. Eco-evangelism requires the church to engage the interlocking systems of exploitation that poison rivers, force children to slave in cigarette factories, give blood diamonds their name, and pump toxins into the air. Eco-evangelism is about redeeming the earth that God made.

Eco-evangelism and the New Atheism

Eco-evangelism must also engage "the new atheism" being preached in the name of "nature."[42] Science and religion, according to proponents of the new atheism, are mutually exclusive. Richard Dawkins's

41. Matthew Sleeth, a former emergency room physician now working as an evangelical environmental activist, uses the term "eco-evangelism" to describe his premise that as Christians take a prophetic stance on behalf of the environment, they become moral leaders in our broken world (Matthew Sleeth, "The Future of Eco-Evangelism," *AlterNet*, April 23, 2005, www.alternet.org/environment/21847?page=2). For more on the relationship of ecotheology to missiology and ecclesiology, see Neil Darragh, "Adjusting to the Newcomer: Theology and Ecotheology," *Pacifica* 13 (June 2000): 160–80.

42. While Richard Dawkins and others claim to be against religion in general, their actual arguments are primarily against Christianity.

Foundation for Reason and Science is out to debunk religion, which Dawkins calls "the God delusion."[43] His book of the same title is a best seller, and Dawkins is not alone. Sam Harris, Daniel C. Dennett, Victor J. Stenger, and Christopher Hitchens are only a handful of militant atheists who are convinced that Christianity is toxic to human life.[44] According to them, Christians use religion to oppress people and nature, and also refuse to acknowledge the truth about the world found in science. The cause of violence, they say, is religion. They are determined to evangelize the world to atheism.

Neuroscience and biochemistry are used to demythologize religious experience, everything from mystical visions[45] to altruism.[46] These spiritual phenomena, we are told, are all subtle forms of genetic adaptation, in one way or another related to the survival of the fittest. Bonaventure's perspective that God works *through* natural phenomena, that God is *revealed* in nature, is not allowed. Woolman's belief that there is no division between natural and supranatural,[47] sacred and secular, is not allowed. The solution to the world's ills in this schema is to expose religion for the utter fraud that it is and embrace "reality," a deterministic, materialistic worldview. Wendell Berry calls this move-

43. http://richarddawkins.net/foundation.

44. See, for example, best sellers with similar themes in Sam Harris, *The End of Faith: Religion, Terror and the Future of Reason* (New York: Norton, 2005); Christopher Hitchens, *God Is Not Great: How Religion Poisons Everything* (New York: Twelve, 2007); and Victor J. Stenger, *God: The Failed Hypothesis, How Science Shows That God Does Not Exist* (Amherst, NY: Prometheus, 2007).

45. The impact of such thinking is found in how religious experience is described in the academy. Kristina Lerman ("The Life and Works of Hildegard von Bingen [1098–1179]," www.fordham.edu/halsall/med/hildegarde.html), for example, comments that "it is now generally agreed" that Hildegard's visions (and by extension the extraordinary spiritual power and creativity that resulted from her mystical experiences) were simply the result of migraine headaches. The reader is left with the impression that if these were migraines then they cannot be taken seriously as visionary gifts. Poor, deluded Hildegard!

46. For a sample of recent discussions in the news, see Jay Tolson, "Is There Room for the Soul?" *U.S. News & World Report*, October 15, 2006, http://health.usnews.com/usnews/health/articles/061015/23soul.htm; Jeffrey Kluger et al., "Is God in Our Genes?" *Time*, October 25, 2004, www.time.com/time/magazine/article/0,9171,995465–3,00 .html; and "Are You a Giver? Brain Scan Tells the Truth," Reuters, www.msnbc.msn .com/id/16740765.

47. By "supranatural" Woolman means something that exists but that at this time lacks precise scientific or natural descriptions or explanations.

ment the "religification and evangelization of science,"[48] with science taking upon itself the stature of the church in the Middle Ages.[49] The erosion of moral constraints on science-and-technology-wed-to-industry is inevitable in such a mechanistic worldview.

Eco-evangelism must respond to these challenges, articulating a robust theology of creation. The church must engage the increasingly complex ethical issues of biotechnology. But even more, we must act. We must inhabit our apologetics in an increasingly mutilated world. The unholy alliance of science, technology, and industry has given birth to monstrous offspring that threaten the very future of the planet. From factory farming to the harvesting of human eggs, commodified science and technology comes with a utilitarian ethic. Life is cheap. Forests, animals, and people are raw materials. Everyone and everything is expendable.[50] Whatever brings the greatest profit is worth the violence.

God is calling the church in the night to retrieve the meaning of stewardship first and foremost as caring for the earth.[51] Evangelism is not good news until it is good news for all of creation, for humanity, animals, plants, water, and soil, for the earth that God created and called good.

Conclusion

Is God green? Is God concerned about the healing of the earth, or only the well-being of souls? What might our mystics say? In the past

48. Wendell Berry, *Life Is A Miracle: An Essay against Modern Superstition* (Washington, DC: Counterpoint, 2000), 19.

49. Ibid., 16.

50. For recent award-winning treatments of these themes, see Eric Schlosser, *Fast Food Nation* (New York: Houghton Mifflin, 2001); *Baraka*, DVD, directed by Ron Fricke (Mpi Home Studio, 2001); and Al Gore, *An Inconvenient Truth*, DVD, produced by Lawrence Bender, Laurie David, and Scott Burns, directed by Davis Guggenheim (Paramount, 2006).

51. Indeed, the belief that stewardship is primarily about money reflects the idol that money has become in the church. Along with many other contemporary theologians, Denis Edwards (*Ecology at the Heart of Faith* [Maryknoll, NY: Orbis, 2006], 25) argues for the use of the phrase "cultivating and caring for creation" rather than "stewardship," because of the many ways in which "stewardship" has been used to justify exploitation.

several chapters we explored many interrelated themes about the love of God that are central to the mystics' understanding of the good news. The remainder of this book describes what it might "look like" for the church to live in a contemplative stance, embodying the love of God described in chapters 2 through 6. As we bring this portion of the book to a close in considering eco-evangelism, let us think about our mystics in a biblical image, "the communion of the saints."

I like to imagine them gathered around a big, oval table, the kind found in farmhouse kitchens in Ohio. The kingdom of God is, after all, a banquet. The conversation goes something like this. Julian of Norwich holds out a hazelnut and tells us she saw creation like that in a vision. Creation was as a tiny hazelnut held in the hands of a loving God. Love is God's meaning, she assures us. It is love that created this world, love that sustains this world, and love that will redeem this world.

It is true, love will have the last word, Hans Urs von Balthasar says. For that reason we have great hope. He looks around the table with a smile.

But God does not force us to be holy, Phoebe Palmer warns. We have choices to make every day about becoming the good news of God's love. We must surrender to the Holy Spirit, the Lord and giver of life. If we put ourselves on the altar we will receive the purity and power we need to take God's love into the world. She reminds us of Five Points Mission.

Father Arseny is quiet, choosing his words slowly. He will always remember the hell of the Soviet work camps. We are here to bear one another's burdens, he says, and thus fulfill the law of Christ. Sometimes we are sent to places we never would choose for ourselves, places that are crimes against nature, worlds of concrete and barbed wire that seem determined to blot out life. But God's life cannot be extinguished, he says. In the camps and prisons we bear the light of Christ. We become the icons of the Lord. There are many obscure Christians in such places, he says. They are the true heroes of our faith.

Thomas R. Kelly recalls his visits to Nazi Germany and agrees with Father Arseny. He tells us how the white-hot love of God opened his eyes to the beauty and vulnerability of the world, how he was liberated from his own ego and striving. He urges us to center down in God's love. There we will clearly discover day by day what we are to do. The blessed community, he says, will help us. We are never alone.

It is true, we are never alone, Henri Nouwen says. We are chosen and beloved, called by Jesus to be taken, blessed, broken, and given. Out of our own wounds and sorrows, the wounded healer tells us, we will find compassion to work for the healing of the world.

Julia Foote remembers her mother's wounds and her own struggle for freedom. She reminds us that we are no longer bound by race, class, or gender. The oppression of slavery and the subjugation of women must have no place among God's children, she cries.

Mechthild of Magdeburg bids us to work among the poor, for there we will find the Christ we love. Do you want to see the face of Jesus? she asks. Then look at the face of the least of these.

Yes, Jesus is found among the poor, Bonaventure says, but he is also seen in the lilies and the stars, in everything he has made. He is the sum of all perfections in the earth.

John Woolman looks around the table, then walks to the door, his arms thrown out wide. "Friends," he calls out, "won't you join me in the task for which we were born, to be channels of liberating love? Come, I will show you the way."

PART THREE

UNION

7

A Hermeneutic of Love

What if we looked at our world as Julian learned to, "with pity and not with blame"? What if we heard God's call to evangelize out of love instead of fear, hope instead of judgment? What if we saw sin for the complex mixture it is, grounded in wounds and unmet needs? What if we automatically tried to see the "total fact" of others? In short, what would it mean to read our world with a hermeneutic of love?

Julian of Norwich and Hans Urs von Balthasar have given us a window through which to see the possibilities. In Julian's Servant Parable we see with clarity that Christ is the second Adam, bound forever in love to humanity.[1] Balthasar teaches us that God's omnipotence means "love-almightiness," a nonpunitive doctrine of atonement in which Jesus has utter solidarity with us in our broken world. But what would it mean for the church to live this way, day to day, in union with the Christ of Julian and Balthasar? In this chapter I will explore this question—how to live through a hermeneutic of love—as the first and central element of a contemplative stance in evangelism.

1. Recall that Julian's vision of the first and second Adam is quite Pauline in its foundation.

The Two Hands of Holiness

There were five of us on the field trip that drizzly morning in June 2007. I was taking students working on their doctor of ministry degree to one of the poorest Latino neighborhoods in Dallas. We drove past shabby bungalows and abandoned cars, stray dogs and cast-off sofas. At last we reached our destination, a nondescript, redbrick building with a long, high carport. Beneath the carport moved a motley group of volunteers filling nearly two hundred grocery bags with food. Later that afternoon, scores of families would come to get their weekly bag of groceries. The front door opened and we were ushered inside by a young Indian woman. She wore the white habit with blue trim that has become a globally recognized icon for Mother Teresa, the late founder of the Missionaries of Charity. "Wait here," she said. "Sister will be with you soon." In the dim light of the foyer we noticed several religious pictures and the words of Jesus from the cross, "I thirst."

We were in the home for unwed mothers, one of several outreach ministries run by the Missionaries of Charity in Dallas. There are currently six hundred Missionaries of Charity communities in the world. The small outpost in Dallas consists of four sisters living in a tiny house a few doors down from the home for unwed mothers. St. James Catholic Church occupies much of the space on the other end of the block. We had come to learn what a women's monastic community could teach us about ecclesiology in a postmodern world. In some ways this experience might prove more valuable to us than a trip to Calcutta, for this little band of women is living in our city, their contemplative vision of evangelism made flesh in acts of love.

After a few moments Sister Salvinette, a small woman, appeared, her large, brown eyes luminous with joy and welcome. I thought about the beauty of her name, with its root meanings of salvation and healing. She, too, is Indian. I pondered Philip Jenkins's and others' forecast that, in the future, missionaries will increasingly come to the United States from the southern and eastern hemispheres, in a reversal of eighteenth- and nineteenth-century trends.

Sister Salvinette led us to the small chapel in the unwed mothers' home, where we were greeted by Sister Marcella, the mother superior for eighteen Missionary of Charity communities in a multistate region.

We were fortunate in having arrived before Sister Marcella's departure that morning. While we faced the altar in the spartan chapel, Sister Marcella gave us a short talk on the spirituality of Mother Teresa, under whose tutelage she had come to embrace her vocation.

"Hold up your right hand," she told us. "Look at each finger. Mother taught us to use our right hand to remember one side of holiness. 'You-did-it-unto-me,' Jesus said. Each word goes with one finger. Try it with me." Like students in vacation Bible school, we all held up our right hand and practiced saying "You did it unto me." While we opened and closed each finger, Sister Marcella spoke in low tones, explaining to us that Jesus is found among people, especially those in need. But regardless of a person's condition, Jesus is there with him or her, and whatever we do to other people, we do to Jesus. Therefore, if we want to love and serve Jesus we must do so by loving and serving other people.

"Now hold up your left hand," she said. Up went our left hands. "I will to want, with God's blessing, to be holy." Each short phrase belonged to its own finger. "I will" was assigned to our thumbs. "'I will' means 'I willingly choose to want holiness,'" Sister Marcella explained. "I want," the index finger, is about wanting to be holy even when one feels unable to do so. "If we freely choose to want to be holy," she said, "God will do the rest." With each phrase she held up another finger. "God will bless us," the middle finger; "to be," the ring finger; "holy," the pinky. "Practice with me," she said, so we did. It was clear that the Missionaries of Charity believed in free will, a theme we explored later with Sister Salvinette. "Put your two hands together," Sister Marcella urged. "These two hands together are what holiness means. On the one hand, we see Jesus in those around us. On the other hand, we choose to submit ourselves to God to love and serve Jesus in those people. It's very simple. Jesus said from the cross, 'I thirst.' You see the words here on the wall. Jesus thirsts in the people around us. We are called to minister to him there."

Soon it was time for Sister Marcella to leave for the airport. She bowed slightly toward us with her hands together, then left. As we waited for Sister Salvinette to come back we practiced putting our hands together for Jesus, saying the words under our breath. I looked across at my students, four United Methodist pastors, each man at least a foot taller than any of the sisters. One of them ventured, "I feel like I need to get smaller. I feel like I'm too big." We were all about to learn the way of getting small.

They Think We Want Something

By the time we made our way back to the carport, most of the volunteers were gone. There was still work to do, bread to be distributed and plastic bags to prepare. While we worked we talked with Sister Salvinette about her life as a Missionary of Charity. My students had prepared lists of questions, which they asked. Each response Sister Salvinette made was like a small earthquake, cracking open our imagination.

The basic ministry, Sister Salvinette told us, is prayer. The sisters gather together four times a day to pray for an hour. They use mostly silent prayer, contemplating the love of God in front of the Blessed Sacrament. This is how they receive the love they need, to give to the people. "We could never do what we do if we did not pray this way," Sister Salvinette told us. "It would be too hard."

She continued, "We go out two by two and knock on doors in the neighborhood. We offer to pray with people and to listen to them talk about whatever is going on in their lives. Sometimes they don't want to talk to us or let us come in. It's always because they think we want something. A donation or money. We tell them no, we are just there to pray for them and get to know them. That is how we basically do our ministry. We find out what they need, what is going on in their lives, and we pray about that with them and try to help them if possible."

Sister Salvinette went on to explain that if people want to donate money, it does not go to the sisters' community in Dallas. Any donations people may give are sent to their order's headquarters, where it is distributed to help support the sisters around the world and to fund ministries like the unwed mothers' home. Many people work with the sisters as volunteers, all of whom are welcome regardless of religious affiliation. But the vast majority of the tasks are carried out by the sisters.

Their ministry is not a social service agency, Sister Salvinette told us. If people need social services, the sisters refer them to the right place. Their weekly food distribution and other acts of charity are simply extensions of their prayer and of being good friends to their neighbors. Prayer is the basis for their lives, she repeated, the main thing they do.

Sometimes my students think it is good to offer neighborly help as a form of evangelism, I told our hostess. But they are reluctant to tell those they are helping that they are doing it because of Jesus or the gospel. They think that offering such kindness in the name of Jesus is coercive toward those they help. This is, after all, a pluralistic world.

Sister Salvinette grew animated. "We would never coerce anyone," she said, "but we always do these things for Jesus, and we tell people about him. Remember, Jesus said that if we are ashamed of him before men, he will be ashamed of us before the Father!" She then told a story of a man she met while knocking on doors in the neighborhood. When she offered to pray for him after talking with him, he refused, saying he didn't believe in prayer or her faith. "That's okay," she answered, "I need prayer for myself so you can just listen while I pray for both of us."

The sisters' lives are very simple, with no television or computers and only one day off per week. Even that day is devoted to prayer by and for the sisters. Each sister has one hour a week for herself, during which time she can garden, read, or rest. Sister Salvinette told us that leisure time leads to a craving for luxury, which leads people away from holiness. I thought about the countless luxuries that mark my own daily life, from French roast coffee to a closet full of clothes. I thought about the church in America, about our craving for luxury as a church. Could it be that we have too much leisure?

When we finished putting the bread in the rows of bagged groceries, then covered it all with tarps, Sister Salvinette gave each of us gifts: a novena with meditations from Mother Teresa, devotional medals, and a wonderful meditation about the thirst of Christ. We drove back to campus marveling at what we had experienced. The Missionaries of Charity in Dallas were light-years ahead of any church of which any of us had ever been a part. They were living a hermeneutic of love.

"What would happen if we actually lived this way?" one student asked.

"I'm thinking about praying with the staff of my church four times a day," another said. "What a difference that would make! I'm trying to even imagine bringing up the possibility. What would the staff say?"

What indeed? The foundation of the sisters' countercultural life is the bedrock conviction that Jesus literally is found in and among other people, especially those who "thirst." Their theology of the immanence of God results in a praxis of charity toward all people. Rather than looking at those outside their community as persons to attract into their order or from whom to get some kind of contribution, the sisters live entirely for the sake of their neighbors, out of love for Christ. One of the most striking features we noticed in our conversation was the sisters' utter lack of fear. These women believe God will take care of them, even as they live and work in a part of the city with one of the highest crime rates in the nation. They are fully aware of social problems, crime, drugs, and every other hazard of their neighborhood. Yet they are not afraid. We asked them if they are ever robbed. Sister Salvinette smiled and said, "We have nothing for anyone to take." She was right. They have nothing, including no fear.

Imagining a New Way

Since I teach evangelism at Perkins School of Theology, I often have opportunities to talk to congregations about evangelism. Dallas is the buckle of the Bible Belt, with many more large churches than in most of the rest of the nation. I often find myself in suburban, upscale congregations talking about ecclesiology. Whenever I talk about a church becoming missional and leaving behind its self-centeredness, when I talk about the poor, invariably I am told that what people like the Missionaries of Charity are doing is fine for them, but not practical for most people. They are a special-interest ministry, not "the church." I am told that the normal church in the suburbs is a building with lots of programming to meet the needs of the members. Evangelism is mostly about strategies to keep newcomers from leaving for another church. Most of these churches have short-term mission trips in the summer, where youth and adults do cross-cultural ministry among the poor. Most of them donate money to local homeless shelters and food banks. These forms of outreach are seen as the church's contribution to mission.

The idea of congregants living like the Missionaries of Charity in our own suburban neighborhoods seems unimaginable. But is it? Is being the church really about buildings, programs, budgets, and "giving units"?[2] Isn't the "normal" church supposed to be a community of Christians living for the sake of the world? What is the basis for our ecclesiology?

The hermeneutic of love is grounded in the belief that Jesus really does live in the people around us, that Jesus thirsts in our actual neighbors. Jesus is bound with eternal love to every person I encounter. This is the starting point. When I see people that way, everything changes. How I evangelize changes. My ecclesiology changes. Now I see people already being called by the Holy Spirit, already being loved and known by Jesus before I ever meet them. Now I understand that prayer and friendship are the foundation for my relationships with others, in the name of Jesus. With a hermeneutic of love I give myself in prayer and friendship to the people around me, not so that I can get something from them, not even a commitment to join my church, but so that I can minister to Jesus in them, Jesus who thirsts.

To do this I have to think about what it means for myself and other people to be sinners. I have to rethink sin, what Luther called the soul curved in on itself, and its relationship to wounds. A hermeneutic of love means that God looks at human sin "with pity and not with blame," because God sees the complexity of sin and wounds. A hermeneutic of love includes a doctrine of atonement that is nonpunitive, meaning Jesus chooses solidarity with us sinners so that he can set us free from sin. When Jesus sets us free, we are free indeed. With the hermeneutic of love I see others' sin the way Jesus does, not as insurmountable obstacles or permanent stains, but as the consequences of life in a broken world. I see the full power of resurrection for them, before it ever happens. This means I believe in the potential for their

---

2. The first time I heard of church members being called "giving units" I thought it was a joke. It is hard to imagine Jesus calling anyone, even the rich young ruler, a "giving unit."

healing as well as their forgiveness. No one is beyond the possibility of being made new in Christ. A hermeneutic of love is fully aware of the devastation of sin and evil, yet refuses to give them the last word.

Sam Goes to Church

To bring this theory into the frontier of the church in postmodern life, in this and subsequent chapters we will imagine a man, Sam, who had been divorced several times. Sam was an accountant living in a large city. Let's think about Sam being invited to First Church by his colleague Bill, who was a member there. First Church was active in evangelism and had dynamic student ministries. Sam agreed to go to church with Bill, thinking his daughter from his first marriage, who was with him every other weekend, might get involved in the youth group and perhaps avoid some of the mistakes he made when he was her age.

First Church considered itself very evangelistic but was strict about divorced people. A divorced person couldn't serve in a spiritual leadership role at First Church. While some denominations had become more gracious toward the divorced, the fact remained that in much of the church world divorced people like Sam experienced judgment and marginalization. This was true regardless of the reason they were divorced. It was true even though at least 50 percent of marriages in the United States today end in divorce.[3] In much of the church today, to be divorced is to be like the woman with the issue of blood in the Gospels,[4] permanently unclean. The divorced person can do nothing to be "cleansed" of the stain of divorce, and the drain on his or her emotions, relationships, finances, and family is staggering. The church's attitude toward divorced persons was based on a particular hermeneutic of Scripture and was an effort to keep church members

3. Since 1997, 50 percent of first marriages and 60 percent of remarriages have ended in divorce in America ("U.S. Divorce Statistics," *Divorce Magazine*, www .divorcemag.com/statistics/statsUS.shtml).

4. Mark 5:21–34. Parallel renderings of the story are found in Matt. 9:18–26 and Luke 8:40–56, but I find the Markan account especially compelling because of its critique of how much the woman had endured, financially and physically, at the hands of the physicians.

from succumbing to the "sin"[5] of divorce. In many ways this logic was like the ritual purity laws that kept the woman with the issue of blood from being allowed to touch her family or friends, attend worship, or have any kind of meaningful social contact for the long years of her affliction. She was no longer human, but a condition, one that might taint the congregation.[6]

Bill was excited that Sam agreed to come to church. He hoped Sam would find Christ and, with the help of new friends who were Christians, be able to stay single. Remarriage after divorce was not an option at First Church. However, when Sam went to church it took only a few weeks before he realized that no matter how much Jesus loved and forgave him for his "sin of divorce," the church would never fully love and forgive him. He would never be allowed to be a deacon, an elder, or a pastor because of his past. He could be baptized and sing in the choir, but he couldn't direct the choir. He could attend Sunday school but never teach it. He could donate money to the church, but he couldn't be a treasurer, all because he had been divorced. Sam didn't aspire to be a deacon or pastor or to lead anything at that point, but he couldn't help wondering what would happen if God should call him to do something in the future. He looked at the men on the platform every week and wondered if they knew anything about suffering.

Sam never heard anyone at the pulpit talk with insight or compassion about the complex reasons people get divorced, or the unhealed wounds that caused people to keep choosing destructive relationships,

5. Usually in these churches there is no critical reflection on the question of whether divorce is always a sin. The possibility that divorce is sometimes necessary to save lives, as in the case of battering relationships, is not allowed. Nor is the fact that one spouse can sin against the other and destroy the marriage, so that a person can truly be the victim rather than perpetrator of sin in a divorce. Like Sabbath laws in the Old Testament, which were intended for the liberation of humans, animals, and the earth, divorce laws were for the protection of vulnerable women and children. And, like Sabbath laws, which have been wrongly used to oppress and condemn God's people, divorce laws in the Bible have been perverted to perpetuate the exclusion and oppression of God's people.

6. For a thorough summary of contemporary discussion regarding the exclusion and alienation of the suffering woman of Mark 5, see Susan Miller, *Women in Mark's Gospel* (New York: T&T Clark International, 2004), 52–53; and Ben Witherington III, *The Gospel of Mark: A Socio-Rhetorical Commentary* (Grand Rapids: Eerdmans, 2001), 184–91.

or the possibility that Jesus could actually heal those wounds and make all things new. He did hear, nearly every week, comments about the loss of family values in America as reflected in the divorce rate, homosexuality, and abortion. Sam wondered about being classified with homosexuals and women who have had abortions. Sam wondered how he was destroying America when he was a veteran and a responsible citizen. Sam's daughter, Jen, liked the youth group a lot, but after several months of church attendance and attempts to fit in at First Church, Sam stopped attending. It was too depressing and demoralizing to be told, week after week, that he was the cause of America's downfall.

What would it look like if First Church embraced a hermeneutic of love, decided to live for the sake of the world, and gave up the false ecclesiology that equates church with buildings, programs, budgets, and giving units? What if First Church looked at Sam and Jen and saw Jesus thirsting? How would things be different for Sam, Jen, Bill, and the rest of the people in this alternative scenario? It might look something like this.

Sam Experiences a Hermeneutic of Love

Bill had a colleague at work named Sam who had been divorced several times. When Bill and Sam talked about life, Sam sometimes expressed loneliness and alienation. He wondered why he kept marrying women who treated him with contempt, then cheated on him and left. He was worried about his daughter, Jen, who was fourteen years old and stayed with Sam only every other weekend. When Sam confided in Bill about his loneliness and his worries about Jen, Bill listened carefully. He remembered what his pastors had taught the congregation about locating every human pain and sorrow in the suffering of Christ. Bill listened to Sam's worries about Jen and recalled Jesus on the cross, asking John to take care of his mother. Jesus was worried about his mother's well-being. As Bill listened to Sam's loneliness he also thought about Jesus asking the disciples if they, too, were planning to abandon him. It had become almost second nature for Bill to think this way, with mercy and without blame.

Bill decided after some time to invite Sam to attend church with him. Sam agreed to go because he had grown to trust Bill, and also because Bill said there were several kids Jen's age. When Sam attended church the first time he was surprised by many things. Even though the congregation was fairly small, he found listed in the bulletin more than a dozen recovery groups. In addition to groups for recovery from various addictions Sam read about a group for divorce recovery, one for healing from shame, one for blended families, and one for healing from sexual abuse. Sam made a mental note to find out what it would cost to go to the groups. The bulletin didn't say. He was also startled to see announcements about other churches in the area from other denominations, for their worship times and Bible studies.

As people gathered for worship Sam noticed that the church was diverse, racially and socially. The sanctuary was on the shabby side, but the feeling of joy was palpable. What touched Sam the most this first Sunday was the sermon, both its content and delivery. The pastor, Clark, read from the Bible a strange story of a woman who had hemorrhaged for twelve years, so she was cut off from society. She felt like her life was a failure and nothing she did could change that. As Clark read and discussed the passage, Sam was drawn into the story.

The woman had spent all her money on healing but the doctors only made her worse. The law was against her, too, Clark said, so that she was unable to touch family or friends because of her condition, which was "ritually impure."[7] She was cut off from family, friends, and the community by this malady that befell her, and she went around all the time feeling doomed. She wasn't even welcome in worship. "There are many of us who know what that is like," Clark said, "who have gone through life feeling unclean, with nowhere else to turn. We're exhausted and broken from our suffering. We feel Godforsaken." Sam was surprised to hear Clark say "we" feel Godforsaken.

7. Notice that all the healings in Mark 5 have to do with purity issues. The demonized man in the tombs, Jairus's daughter, and the woman represent the three kinds of uncleanness that, according to Num. 5:1–5, required persons to be excluded from the community: those with skin diseases or bodily discharges and those who touched a corpse. Thus Mark emphasizes the dynamic power of Jesus to heal every form of impurity that excludes people from the faith community (Miller, *Women in Mark's Gospel*, 55).

Godforsaken is right, Sam thought. Did Clark know about his failed life? Sam glanced around and saw other people nodding their heads, some wiping away tears. An elderly black woman leaned forward and said, "Come on pastor, come on, tell us." She was wearing a violet dress with a matching hat. Her eyes were ancient and wrinkled with hard times.

"Jesus doesn't see the woman the way everyone else does," Clark said. "Jesus looks at her with love and compassion. She is a daughter of Abraham, a member of the family, someone worthy of respect. Instead of her uncleanness polluting Jesus, his goodness makes her whole. Jesus is glad to touch her. The woman goes away standing tall, ready to start living her new life. This is what Jesus does for all of us." A fine mist of sweat broke out on Clark's forehead. The church wasn't air-conditioned. "He looks at us with compassion and hope. There are so many ways we fall into a ditch. We get bruised and crippled. We can't see." He was rhythmic now, his words coming in a cadence. The woman in violet moved with him, crying "Amen" and "Preach it."

"How can any of us know why another person falls?" Clark asked. "We are a complex mixture of wounds and needs and sin. We have been born into a world that is already broken, so we get broken, too. The good news of the gospel"—the woman raised her hand and waved it, her upturned face lost in praise—"is that Jesus forgives our sins and heals our wounds. He makes us into new people, transforming us from the inside out."

Sam began to feel, for the first time in his life, that God might actually love him. He wished for a moment that he could touch Jesus, just like the woman in the story. Then the feeling passed. Later, over lunch, he asked Bill about the sermon. "I never heard a religious leader speak with such compassion about people most churches reject. That preacher actually gives hope."

Bill replied with a broad smile, "First Church is all about being made new in Christ. Clark is no stranger to pain," he added. "For that matter, every pastor in this church has a story of redemption. Why not ask Clark to tell you his story sometime? He's a very hospitable man. He'll welcome the chance to talk."

8

Giving Ourselves Away

The two hands of holiness mentioned by Sister Salvinette in chapter 7 have to be open, reaching out. Being open, they are unable to cling. A contemplative stance means a basic posture of openness, a willingness to be present without grasping. But like an old woman with dementia the church in the night shuffles wild-eyed through the halls of daily life, clutching a little basket full of things. Kenosis is the life of letting go, of putting our basket and ourselves on the altar. The church must come to understand that its vocation is about giving instead of getting, and Phoebe Palmer and Father Arseny are the guides who show us the way.

From Palmer we learn that the way of holiness is a way of surrender, not so that we can receive a religious experience, but so that God can give redeeming love through us, to the world. Palmer opens the door for us to enter the path of holiness by showing us how to put all that we are and all that we have on the altar of Jesus. This includes the losses and the mysteries of the dark night. Jesus will make us holy. Nothing of our lives will be wasted or lost.

Father Arseny's Orthodox tradition taught him that the priestly vocation is essentially one of kenosis. But for Father Arseny the priestly vocation was lived in a "parish" assigned by a communist regime. After spending years of his life pursuing an education, first in the university, then through his theological training, life took a dreadful turn. There would be no village or church or monastery for Father Arseny. Yet he did not stop being a priest. Father Arseny lived his vocation in the camps, among "the least of these." He became "the least of these." Day after day, year after year, he loved people for Jesus in a hell only humans could design. He was like Jesus, descending to the pit in solidarity with the damned. Through him the word was made flesh, and Jesus was born again in many hearts.

It is a challenge for American clergy to relate to Father Arseny or to Phoebe Palmer. We think of them as rare anomalies in the realm of Christian service. Even the Missionaries of Charity seem like a special interest group. We do not think of church in terms of kenosis, or open hands, or a corporate, nongrasping presence. We don't imagine giving ourselves as a whole offering, in the manner of Palmer. Nor do we cultivate in seminarians the sense that their vocation is essentially one of kenosis, in the manner of Father Arseny. We do not teach our congregations that kenosis is the normal Christian life. Instead, we teach people to give money. Our goal is to bring them to the point of tithing, because the average church member in America contributes only 2 percent of his or her income.

The hunger for success is so seductive. Numbers, buildings, revenue, honors, being called the Reverend Doctor, being known as the Tall Steeple Church—these are the kinds of temptations, Father Arseny warned, that lead to demonic oppression.[1] The clergy who were eager to advance themselves in such ways in Father Arseny's time were the ones most easily manipulated by the government to inform on their fellow clergy in the Russian church. Father Arseny and others like him were sent to camps in no small part because of the jealousy and competitive spirit of colleagues who were eager to get ahead.

In the United States the temptation is not so different. We do not think of our neighbors and hear Jesus say, "I thirst." Instead we think of giving units, salaries, health insurance, new sanctuaries, cutting-edge music, and the big church that is taking all our young people with

---

1. Bouteneff, *A Cloud of Witnesses*, 56, 100.

its dynamic youth pastor and exciting trips. How can we ever compete with that? we ask ourselves. We just are not entertaining enough.

What would it mean if pastors, like Jesus in the wilderness, resisted the logic of the tempter? What if they led the church to do the same? What if we lived the kenotic hymn?[2]

A Way That Is Not So New

The idea is really not so new. The Quakers originally had no paid clergy. Instead, the people shared the ministry, and those who were gifted to preach, like John Woolman, preached. The Quakers have always had an impact on the world much larger than their numbers seem to warrant. They have been at the forefront of human rights activism around the world, and they have done it in the name of Jesus, without pay. Thus in Quaker tradition we have one historic model of kenosis.

The early Methodist societies were in many ways semimonastic communities for ordinary lay people. The emphasis was on holiness of heart and life, a combination of personal piety and social activism, which was essentially a posture of kenosis. Methodism became the largest Christian movement in North America by the mid-nineteenth century because of the power of its class and band meetings to form Christian disciples. Class and band leaders were unpaid laity. Many holiness Methodists were unpaid lay leaders whose social justice advocacy reformed American culture. Palmer, for example, never received payment for her ministry, not even for travel expenses. This was a historic Methodist model of kenosis.

Many other examples could be given from Christian history, from the Beguines, the Franciscans, and the Plymouth Brethren, to name just a few. Some of these were monastic orders, some were lay movements, both Catholic and Protestant. In each case Christians understood holiness as a call to kenosis, to living as broken bread and poured out wine for the world. Because we are surrounded by this great cloud of witnesses, we know that we can live this way today. When the church has embraced kenosis, the results have always been powerful. The

2. Phil. 2:1–11.

church has been at its missional best when giving itself away. Kenosis is not a utopian dream. It is the way the church is supposed to be.

Bivocational Pastors

One model of kenosis for today could be small, missional congregations led by teams of bivocational pastors. The pastors would earn their living with ordinary jobs like anyone else, as teachers, nurses, dentists, auto mechanics, and the like. This would not be a temporary situation until the church became "self-supporting"; it would be the permanent arrangement. The team of pastors would rotate preaching responsibilities and share pastoral care. With each pastor being a shepherd for just twenty to thirty people, the time required would be manageable.

The pastor's primary task would be the cultivation of community and the spiritual formation of the congregation, who would be equipped and deployed into their neighborhoods to be a blessing. Rather than the church focusing its energy and resources on itself (pastors' salaries and benefits, big buildings with massive utility bills, programs to keep church members happy), the church would focus its resources outward in service. The fruitful church would give birth to new, similarly small and simple congregations, also led by teams of bivocational pastors.

This model of church would be especially adaptable to urban and rural settings, places that are studiously avoided by many church developers today. After all, it is far more profitable to launch a new church in an upscale new suburb than among the working poor. This model could also work wonders in suburban America where people live in the same neighborhood for years without knowing any of their neighbors. The kenotic church could reintroduce the practice of community, with wide-ranging spiritual and social effects.

The model of bivocational pastor has always existed in poor urban settings, especially in the African-American church. Yet it has not been seen as a model to emulate, because it is linked to serving the poor and to serving small churches. It's not about getting ahead.

The world needs to see a church that is not all about itself. Sister Salvinette's neighbors sometimes won't open the door because they assume the sisters have come to ask for money. That is the way people in general think of the church today, that what we want is their money. It is our fault that people think that way. We have given them good reason to close their doors. We have, in fact, seen them as giving units, as bodies to fill the new sanctuary and to keep the ship afloat. The only thing that will change this indictment is for the church to become kenotic. The change has to begin with pastoral leadership.

Theological Education

What about theological education for the bivocational pastor? In many mainline denominations pastors can't be ordained without advanced theological degrees. Regardless of denominational requirements, adequate theological education is essential for pastors. This is increasingly true in our pluralistic, globalized world. But is it realistic to expect working adults, many of whom are married and have children, to invest time, money, and energy in a theological education that is not for their own financial gain?

It is if the church is about kenosis. In this model the pastor would not view his or her theological education as a professional degree that will be rewarded with monetary gain. Instead, the whole process would be understood kenotically. If a congregation is not paying for pastors' salaries and expensive buildings, some of the giving could be used for theological education. The pastor would use his or her education, in turn, to equip the congregation. The church would be, in a sense, paying for its own theological education so that it is able to give itself to the world.

Most seminaries have already made significant changes in recent decades to meet the needs of today's working students. Whereas in the past seminary students were usually single and straight out of college, today most seminarians are in their thirties or older and come to seminary from the workforce. Most of them have full- or part-time jobs and families to support. Online classes, shorter intensive classes, and classes that meet once a week have all come about to accommodate today's working students. While more changes need to be made to bring theological education into postmodern realities, it is already possible to get a good theological education from an accredited institution while working and supporting a family. Also, numerous alternative or "underground" seminaries have been formed to equip leaders in the emerging church, a trend that reflects the democratization of knowledge and a resistance to institutional controls.[3] These new kinds of seminaries could resource some bivocational pastors.

Sometimes a story is more useful than anything to help us imagine a new possibility. With that in mind, let's return to Sam, whom we met in chapter 7.

What Do You Do with the Offering?

Several months had passed since Sam's first time in worship. Each Sunday he was surprised by something else, some new liberation of spirit. By now he had heard each of the pastors preach for a month. That's what they did at First Church: each pastor took a month at a time. They were so different from one another. Sylvia loved the minor prophets. She preached with fire and conviction, bringing their message to life for the congregation. Mike knew every alternative band from the last ten years, and now he knew Jen, and Jen trusted him. Kim was the mystic of the four. When she prayed Sam felt himself lean forward, attentive and eager, like his Jack Russell before a walk.

Clark was unlike anyone Sam had ever known. The best way to describe him was by the effect he had on people. When Sam was a boy he would lie on his back in the field on summer days and sink into the waving grass. He would watch clouds form and dissolve and the sun dappling through the trees, intoxicated with the fragrance of the hot earth. At times he felt his heart overwhelmed with the joy of it. Something about Clark's teaching had the same effect, reaching back into some hidden place of dreams and longing. Sam didn't speak of this to Bill or Jen; he wasn't ready. But something was breaking loose inside.

3. One example is the People's Seminary, a ministry of Tierra Nueva in Burlington, WA (www.peoplesseminary.org/ThePeoplesSeminary.html). Three levels of courses are offered, two of which are geared for lay people who are not in a formal seminary program.

The church, he discovered, was more about relationships and community than the worship service. People met in the pastors' homes once a week for a potluck dinner and Bible study. Fifteen or twenty people of various ages usually crowded in. It reminded Sam of his childhood, when his family and all his aunts, uncles, and cousins would go to Grandma's house for dinner. The church potlucks were like that, rowdy times of laughter and honest conversation. They always had communion at the end. Sam felt himself relaxing, ever so slowly. He and Bill go to the group that meets at Clark's house.

One day Sam asked Bill how a congregation so small could support four pastors. "They don't get salaries," Bill said with a laugh. "Sometimes we try to pay them but they won't let us. They're funny that way." Sam was shocked, his face almost comical. "But how do they earn a living?" he asked, truly mystified.

Bill explained that Clark used to be a "normal" pastor with a salary from a church, but some things happened in his life that led him to believe he should pastor without pay. "It's a long story," Bill said. "He'll tell you about it if you ask him. Now he teaches US history at Martin Luther King School. That's his ministry to the kids. Sylvia works at a battered women's shelter. They don't pay much but she has health insurance and she can't imagine going somewhere else.

"But get this," Bill continued, a look of mischief in his eyes. "Mike works for IBM and his wife Libby is a teacher. They used to have a big house and a very comfortable life. You know, sushi dinners and ski vacations. At that time Mike wasn't a pastor. They were in a formation group that Sylvia led and that read Barbara Ehrenreich's *Nickel and Dimed* and some books by Jim Wallis. I think they read John Woolman too." Sam nodded as if he knew the authors, none of whom he'd ever read.

"Anyway, the group agreed to fast and pray for a week to help them discern what kind of changes they could make to live more faithfully in light of what they learned from those readings," Bill said. "A number of them did things like start to use public transportation instead of cars, increase their giving to local missions, that sort of thing. But the biggest change was that Mike and Libby felt called to downsize and simplify. They sold their big house and moved to a working-class neighborhood. As you might imagine, people thought they were nuts to sell their house and move. Even I thought so. But they really felt they had to do it. They put their kids in the neighborhood public school. With the money they've saved by simplifying they've been able to sponsor some underprivileged kids' college tuition and part of Mike's tuition for seminary. They ran a summer program for kids in the neighborhood this year and are doing other things there to build community.

"I have to confess, I've been thinking about doing something like that myself now that I see the difference it's made in that neighborhood," Bill said. "And Mike and Libby are happy. Their kids are doing fine, too. Let's see, that was Clark, Sylvia, and Mike. Oh, and Kim is a dental assistant. None of the pastors make much money, but they get by."

Sam struggled to take it in. A church that gives instead of takes? People who choose to live among the poor when they could be rich? And who were Jim Wallis and John Woolman? Was this some kind of cult? No, it couldn't be. The congregation was part of a mainline denomination that had been around for ages. That's where it got its old building with its old name, First Church. Besides, Bill was a normal guy, Sam thought, a good ten years younger than Sam but still an accountant working at the same firm.

"But what do they do with the offering," Sam finally asked, "if they don't use it for the church?"

"We help people," Bill replied. "That's what we're about."

Living the Kenotic Hymn

Sam settled into the threadbare wingback. The coffee shop was cluttered and familiar, board games stacked in the corner, the air thick with Sumatra, the featured roast. By now the morning crowd had gone so it was reasonably quiet, a good place to finally ask some questions.

Clark came in a few minutes later, his gray hair windblown and a paper tucked under his arm. "Hey," he said with an easy smile. A few minutes later he was sitting across the table. Clark never seemed to rush. It was one of the things Sam noticed about him, that he seemed to bring peace into a room just by being there.

"So, Sam, it's great to have you and Jen with us. You're still pretty quiet at our crazy potluck dinners and Bible studies, but I can always feel the intensity of your listening," Clark said.

Sam laughed. "Yes," he said, self-consciously. "I guess I am a little intense." Some part of him kept wondering when the pressure would come to join, to believe, to do something he didn't want to do. He paused, wondering if he should really say what was on his mind. "It's just that I've never experienced anything like First Church. My family didn't go to church when I was growing up. It seemed pretty irrelevant to my parents. I went to church for a while after my first divorce, but it wasn't like your church at all. It was more normal."

The wrinkles around Clark's eyes deepened with amusement.

"Sorry, that didn't come out right. What I mean is, it was your typical church with a senior pastor and choir and a big building and a capital campaign, all of that."

"I know what you mean." Clark said. "It's okay. We are a little, shall we say, eccentric." They both laughed.

Sam continued. "The pastor seemed like a good guy when he talked to me one-on-one, but from the pulpit he often talked about family values and how this country is falling apart because of divorce, homosexuals, and abortion, and after a while I just couldn't go there anymore. I felt like there was a neon light above my head that said 'Sin.' I don't think he meant anything against me personally. But it was getting to Jen, too, hearing how her dad was responsible for destroying America."

Sam looked at Clark carefully, waiting for his reaction to the words "first divorce." But Clark looked the same, steady and peaceful, kind. No judgment. Another one of those surprises, another freedom. Sam decided to plunge ahead.

"Look, I've been divorced three times and I don't know what is wrong with me," he said. "I don't think I'm that hard to live with. I'm a decent guy for the most part. Sure I've never been very religious, but I support my daughter and I do believe in God. I like a cigar now and then with a glass of Scotch. Those are probably my worst vices. Other than being divorced three times." He paused again, trying to read Clark's face. *Might as well continue,* he thought. *I've already gone this far.*

"What I don't understand is why I never see it coming. I meet a woman, she seems vivacious and charming, we fall in love. We get married, and before you know it she's mad all the time, drinking, abusive. She's gone all night, she says ugly, hateful things. I keep trying to please her, trying to win her back, trying to get help for her. The next thing I know she's having an affair, and then it's over. I can take the drinking and anger, but I can't take the affairs. I don't know what's wrong with me, that I keep doing this to myself. And to Jen."

The words whirled out in a rush, like a balloon suddenly untied. He looked down and to the left while he talked, studying the pattern on the rug. The moment he finished he regretted having spoken and wished that he'd never met Clark or gone to First Church. Bill was the only person he had ever talked to like this, and even with Bill there were things he just never said. He looked up, ready to make an excuse to leave. Then he saw Clark's eyes, filled with compassion.

"My God," Clark said quietly after a while. "You've been through hell. I can't imagine what you've had to endure."

Sam was stunned. Mercy was more unnerving than judgment. He heard himself saying, "Bill told me you're no stranger to pain. He said you have a story of redemption. He actually told me I should ask you about it."

Clark shifted in his chair and took a drink of coffee. "Sam," he said gently, "I just want you to know that you are welcome at First Church. We feel like you and Jen are family. I'm so sorry for the cruelty you experienced from us Christians. We were wrong. You have suffered so much, and we only made it worse.

"I won't go into all the details, as it is a long story, but my wife died from suicide," Clark said. "Losing her was the most painful thing I ever experienced. It made me question the existence of God, my call, everything having to do with my faith, my worth as a human being. I felt like a failure because I hadn't been able to prevent her death. I walked away from the church for a while because it was too painful. I couldn't take the pat answers from well-intentioned church people, or the judgmental attitudes from others. Some churches teach that if you commit suicide you automatically go to hell. My theology was inadequate to handle this kind of loss. So I walked away. I went back to teaching high school, which is what I did before going into the ministry," Clark said.

"After a while I began to think about some of the mystics I read about in seminary, about their spiritual experiences and how they approached life. So many of them suffered terribly and lived in dreadful times in history. Some of them wrote about a spiritual experience called the dark night of the soul, and I vaguely remembered that their description of the dark night was something like what was happening to me. Even though I tried to forget about God and faith, I kept remembering stories from the Gospels. It was kind of like Jesus was following me around not letting me forget him, try as I might. I especially remembered the story of his suffering."

Clark shifted in his chair and continued. "The idea kept coming to me that I should go on a retreat to spend time in prayer. I really wanted to reconnect with God if I could. So I scheduled a week's retreat at a monastery. While I was there I was able to join the monks when they gathered for corporate prayer. There was a beautiful rhythm to their lives, based around their practice of contemplative prayer. I found it very healing. I met with one of them for spiritual conversation once a day. He said I was on track with my thinking that I might be in a dark night of the soul. He was incredibly kind and helpful.

"When I came home I started trying to follow a pattern of daily prayer like the monks, although I had to modify it because of my job. It made me think about how much more effective my life would have been as a pastor if I had followed that kind of practice. I was lucky if I prayed once a day back then."

Sam was amazed at Clark's honesty. He had wondered during his previous church experience if the pastor had known anything about suffering. Clark not only admitted to his mistakes as a pastor, but he talked to Sam as if he was a respected friend. He seemed so normal, like Bill or some other friend. Yet there was something about him that was still elusive to Sam. Something whole and free, something deep.

"I also thought about the monks' commitment to poverty, chastity, and obedience," Clark said. "Their giving of themselves to the world in prayer and service was powerful. It made me think a lot about how we could do church differently if we followed some of those practices. I remembered how exhausted I used to get, trying to raise money for remodeling the sanctuary and for ongoing operating expenses, including my health insurance and pension. I always felt conflicted about that, as if the church existed to support me, when the church is supposed to exist to bless the world.

"A few weeks later I ran into an old friend from seminary, Kim. We were both at a street fair downtown. I hadn't seen her in ages and didn't know she was still in town. I found out that Kim had her own trials, not like mine, but painful. Kim used to be in a different denomination, one that isn't very welcoming of women pastors. I was really shocked to learn she was now a dental assistant. Don't get me wrong, it's a fine profession. But Kim was born to be a spiritual leader. She has incredible gifts of prayer and discernment." Sam nodded his agreement, thinking about the way Kim seemed to know people's hearts when she prayed.

"She just couldn't take the patriarchy anymore in the church," Clark said. "She had been on staff at a large church as a children's pastor. I guess things were pretty toxic. For her own mental health she needed to get out. I'm not telling you anything she won't tell you herself. She tells about her journey fairly often, in different settings."

Sam was startled to hear Clark use the word "patriarchy." Clark seemed like such a regular guy, not some kind of political spokesperson. In fact, none of the pastors appeared to be militant activists. But now that he thought about it, Sam saw that at First Church men and women led together as equals. They just did it without making a big statement about it.

Clark's voice broke into his thoughts. He was saying something about Kim and spiritual disciplines, whatever those were. "Anyway, I told her about my retreat at the monastery and how it made me rethink my understanding of church. We ended up talking about ministry and how amazing it would be to start a new congregation, one that was accepting of people like us who had been kicked around by life. We could actually incorporate into the church some of the monastic practices we found so healing. Kim was very excited about that, as you can imagine, with her strength in prayer and spirituality. That conversation led to many others and eventually gave birth to First Church. Or I should probably say, First Church as we now know it."

"I wanted to ask you about that," Sam said, pulling a worship bulletin from his pocket. "You have some great recovery groups and neighborhood ministries. Bill told me none of you get paid for what you do as pastors. I've never heard of such a thing. Maybe I'm wrong, but I always thought the church was after something, like my wallet for example. Between that and the fact that I'm destroying America, I haven't gotten too much out of religion. But now I have so many questions. I hardly know where to begin." Sam laughed, realizing to his surprise that a burden had lifted. He had confessed his terrible secret to Clark and nothing had changed. Clark was treating him exactly the same. Now they were talking about the church as if Sam and Clark had always been friends.

Clark laughed then, a big belly laugh that filled the room with joy. "Ask away," he said. "But let's take a walk while we finish the conversation. I need to head toward the hospital to see some people."

The New Old First Church

"First Church has been around for eighty-five years," Clark said as they walked out into the morning sun. "It used to be the church to go to if you were somebody. Then the plant closed and the neighborhood began to change. The original members moved out to the suburbs but kept coming back down to church. They didn't know how or didn't want to connect with the new people in the neighborhood. Too many cultural differences, I guess. Anyway, the congregation declined until there were just a handful of elderly members praying for a miracle. The conference was going to close the church and sell the building. It just wasn't feasible to keep it open anymore, the church was in such terrible financial shape.

"That was about the time Kim and I began to talk about a different kind of church. We started out talking about a nondenominational church so we could structure it the way we felt best, without the headache of bureaucratic red tape from a denomination. But the more we talked and prayed about it, the more we kept coming back to my denomination, which is now Kim's too. We loved the theological heritage of the tradition. We wanted to be connected with a church with historic roots, for accountability and to connect us with

the larger church. We decided to present a proposal to the conference for a different model of church. What harm could it do? If the
conference didn't go along with it, we could still think about doing
it on our own."

Clark continued, "Basically what we proposed was a church with
a team of bivocational pastors who were theologically well-educated,
but whose income would come from nonchurch jobs. We loved the
idea of using as much of people's giving as possible to serve the
neighborhood instead of ourselves. By doing the ministry in a team
we could develop a strong church that would not be overly taxing on
any one of us in terms of time and energy. We could share preaching,
teaching, and pastoral care. We could truly equip the congregation
to do the ministries that would emerge from their spiritual gifts and
be of service to the people in the neighborhood. It would be a core
value for us to find as many ways as possible to be present and active
in the neighborhood outside the church and to avoid focusing ministries on ourselves. We would resist unnecessary bureaucracy in the
church as much as we could, just keep it simple. We agreed that if
the church grew much larger than one hundred fifty we would plant
a second church using the same model. Our goal in multiplying the
churches would be to reach neighborhoods like this one, where the
old churches were dying.

"From the very beginning we were committed to practicing a rule
of life together as pastors, and we would teach our congregation to
do the same. That meant a daily prayer practice, not as rigorous as
the monks at St. Michael's, but a definite structure for the day, based
on prayer. We also wanted to function with mutual accountability
and shared power. There would not be a hierarchy. You may have
noticed that none of us is the 'senior pastor.' And we decided that we
would model the kind of ethnic and gender diversity that exists in our
neighborhood, so that people would feel this was their church. God
had already given us a good start in that I'm a white guy and Kim is
Asian. Eventually we added Sylvia, then Mike. The church helped pay
for Sylvia's and Mike's seminary classes when it became clear that
they had the gifts and call to pastoral ministry."

Sam had noticed the diversity the first time he visited. But the diversity was like the patriarchy issue. No one talked about it a lot; the church just seemed to be diverse.

"It took a few weeks for Kim and me to iron out the details of the original plan, but when it was finished we fasted and prayed, then took it to the bishop," Clark said. "We explained that I wanted to be appointed to old First Church, which was about to close, and that we wanted to use this model of church. The bishop was really surprised. She asked us several times about salaries, benefits, and pensions. She was worried about the fact that I am ordained in our denomination and there are so many rules about appointments and salaries for our clergy. In general, bivocational ministry is not part of the picture.

"We kept telling her that we didn't want to earn a living by serving as pastors at First Church. We just wanted to be the church in that neighborhood and lead people to Christ there. We assured her that we would teach the people to give generously, and that we would send a regular contribution to the denomination to support our larger missions nationally and around the world. She seemed especially interested in our plan to follow a rule of life. She said she would need time to think it over.

"To our great joy the bishop called a few weeks later and said the conference was ready to give it a try, as a pilot project. We would be responsible for the utility bills and upkeep of the building and for developing the church in the model we presented. The conference was willing to try this new model because nothing else was working in our denomination to develop churches in our part of the city. So that is how we got started. That was about ten years ago. We are a big experiment in being a church that gives itself away in Jesus's name.

"And here we are at the hospital," Clark said. "I'll see you on Sunday. Remember to bring hot dogs and buns. We're throwing a cook-out for the neighborhood."

9

Homing Prayer

It was a muggy Sunday morning, and I had just come out of the county jail. The Lew Sterritt Justice Center was being enlarged, so the normal entrance was blocked. To get up to the front doors you had to climb a long series of switchbacks, metal ramps built on steel scaffolds. It was as if you were ascending an ancient ziggurat where humans are sacrificed to gods. The ramps jiggled and swayed as streams of worried people went up and down. I had been there to see a friend who had gotten into some trouble.

As I stepped off the last stretch of scaffolding onto the littered sidewalk I noticed a small dog. She was hot and confused, frightened by the traffic and the people milling around. The jail was in a seedy part of town: industrial, a wilderness of concrete, asphalt, and liquor stores. I could see no houses where a little dog might live. As I moved to the crosswalk and waited for the light to change, I was surprised to find her beside me, heeling, her nose tapping against the back of my knee. When I walked, she walked. When I stopped, she sat down, a model of good behavior. She followed me across six lanes of traffic and then a large parking lot filled with cars. Tap, step, tap, step. When I came to my car she stood by the door, ready to get in. I looked at her flea-bitten, scrawny little self. She gazed back into my eyes, hopeful, anxious, tired. I was under her spell. She has been with us ever since.

I learned a few days later when I took her to the vet that the Society for the Prevention of Cruelty to Animals is two blocks from the jail, and people often dump animals there when the office is closed. Though it has been awhile since Bonnie joined our family, she is still in the process of coming home. She is haunted by ghosts of whatever happened in her first twelve months of life. Her face lifts toward me every few seconds when we go for walks, her nose touching my hand. She follows me through the house from room to room. Her bed is beside my desk where she can touch her nose to my foot. When I leave the house she stays at the door, waiting for my return. Each time I come back, even if all I did was take the garbage out, Bonnie squirms with joy and relief.

Bonnie reminds me of us Christians. She is trying so hard to believe the truth that surrounds her, that she is home at last, that we completely love her with all her funny quirks and mongrel beauty. But fear and memories and the mystery of her past are like voices telling her not to believe what she now experiences. It is a struggle. She is slowly gaining trust in our love, and as she does her real personality shows through. She forgets to be afraid, forgets about vigilance, and is just Bonnie. Sometimes she risks a nap in the kitchen instead of my office. Then she wakes up and dashes back to see if I am in my office, and when I am she is ecstatic. In this gradual, halting way, Bonnie is coming home to love.

Like Bonnie, we bring to the work of ministry our own "first twelve months of life." The false self is firmly in place by the time we get to seminary, and for most of us, theological education makes it only worse. Like Henri Nouwen and Thomas R. Kelly, we are schooled in systems that reward the striving of the false self and suppress the one thing needful. Seminaries are not, as a rule, organized around prayer, nor are they focused on the pedagogy of the soul. Most seminaries do not help us to map our journeys, find the sacred gifts in the conflicts of our lives,[1] or cultivate authenticity. For students, mainline theo-

1. I appreciate the playful wisdom of Bishop Hee-Soo Jung, who describes conflict as one of God's best gifts to us because it provides opportunities for growth and change (Hee-Soo Jung, "Hospitality in the Midst of Conflict: God's Grace and Our

logical education in America is overwhelmingly concerned with critical scholarship, with passing Greek vocabulary tests, and with knowing the names of popes and schisms. For many students seminary is like any other school, a matter of competition, grades, saying what the professor wants to hear, and making it through hoops in order to be ordained. It is possible to earn a master's of divinity degree with high honors without having formed habits of prayer or discernment or any spiritual discipline that cultivates inner freedom or that opens us to what Pentecostals call "the anointing." Such matters are ephemeral, the logic goes, not measurable in the world of the academy. Thus prayer and spiritual habits do not fit well, much less belong at the center of the seminary experience, shaping all else that happens.

Pastors formed in this system arrive at the church, diploma in hand, and find themselves in the formidable world of politics, budgets, and boards. Nothing in seminary has prepared us for the brutal conflicts, the low self-esteem of declining congregations, the jockeying for power by men and women who think they own the church.

We have not learned in our families of origin or our home churches to see conflict as a gift from God, so we do not know how to lead the congregation through it. We have been shaped by our own "first twelve months of life." We have not come home yet to our unexamined wounds and undiscovered beauty, to practices that steep us daily in the love of God and lead us to become our true selves. So we respond to the church from the false self, the only thing we know how to do. Like Bonnie outside of the jail, we turn around and around, trying to decide whether to fight or run away.

Seasoned pastors who have been at it for a while are often no better for their experience. The church in the night is tooled to ce- ment the false self into place, especially in the pastor. Systems of rewards and punishments, advancement and withholding, all work together to promote "success" as measured in budgets, buildings, and membership rosters. The pastor's worth is found in ever-increasing productivity measured according to this system. In this situation we are at the mercy of our egos and the competitive, fearful, shaming

Practice," lecture presented at the Spiritual Leaders Conference, Nashville, TN, July 31, 2007).

voices within. What is true of the individual pastors is also true for the church. We become, as Ephesians 4:14 says, tossed and driven, divided within ourselves and against one another.

It does not have to be this way. God does not mean for church to be this way. Through contemplative prayer we can find the path toward healing. I have come to think of it as "homing" prayer. This kind of prayer leads me home to God and to my true self, and it opens ways for me to welcome others into the home of my life. Ultimately, contemplative prayer leads to hospitality, the radical mercy of God extended in human community.

Returning to our narrative of Sam, let's imagine how it might be if pastors were grounded in this kind of prayer, and if they taught the church to be that way too. Through Sam's unfolding journey, perhaps we can picture how a person being evangelized might experience pastors whose central practice is contemplative prayer, and how the church is shaped by these commitments. Sam and his new friends at First Church can help us see the path from prayer to hospitality, the context for healing the threefold wound.

Outward Bound for the Soul

Sam arrived at the lodge early, never having been to a retreat before and not quite sure what to expect. It didn't matter that Kim had explained this would be a retreat introducing some basic forms of prayer, or that he had read about the retreat center on the Web. The truth was, Sam was worried that he might be expected to pray out loud, and he just couldn't do that. Maybe some day, but not now. No one had tried to coax him into anything he didn't want to do at First Church, but he still felt awkward each time he took another step toward the faith that was so real for his new friends.

Pulling his duffle bag from the trunk of the car, he looked around and took a deep breath, letting it out slowly. He waved across the parking lot at two people he recognized from church. The sun was low enough by now to cast long shadows through the pine trees. The rustic lodge was nestled against the hill, flanked by rhododendrons and mountain laurel. Sam's gaze eagerly took in the trail that disappeared up into the woods. Kim had said they would have plenty of time for recreation, that it was essential for a real retreat. His eyes followed the trail down to the boat house at the edge of Painted Lake. *No matter what happens with the prayer stuff,* he thought, *I'm going to love being out on the lake.* His rod and tackle were ready.

Kim was already inside with a helper, making last-minute adjustments to the seating arrangements in the great room. Fifteen people had signed up for the weekend retreat, some of them newcomers to First Church, like Sam, and some who had been around for a while. Half an hour later they were all in the dining hall where dinner was served family style. The long table was loaded with mounded platters of meat loaf and chicken, bowls full of mashed potatoes and salads, heaps of fresh biscuits, and for dessert, peach cobbler. Conversation was lively, punctuated with laughter, just like the weekly potluck dinners. Sam felt his anxiety begin to subside.

When dinner was over participants returned to the great room for the retreat's opening session. "Prayer is like a journey through the wilderness," Kim began. "You watch, you listen, you climb, you get tired and rest, sometimes you don't know which way to go, sometimes it's dark and foggy, and sometimes all you can do is weep at the beauty you find." Sam remembered again his childhood out on the farm, how connected he felt to the earth and weather.

"We are going to use one wilderness story as our guiding text for this whole retreat," Kim continued. "We'll keep coming back to it, looking at it through different lenses. It's a story about a man named Jacob. He was one of the big three, Abraham, Isaac, and Jacob, the great patriarchs of the Old Testament. Only he wasn't so great. Like most of the other heroes of the Bible, he had major issues."

Sam was instantly drawn in. A hero of the Bible with issues?

Kim's eyes twinkled as she smiled at Sam. Sometimes he could swear she could read his mind. "You are probably familiar with some parts of his story even if you never read the Bible," Kim said. "He's the guy who smooth-talked his older brother, Esau, into trading his inheritance for a bowl of beans. He also tricked his father into giving him Esau's blessing. He was a classic mama's boy who pulled some of his sneaky stunts with her help."

Sam laughed out loud, along with everyone else. Why hadn't anyone ever told him the Bible was like this? He could hardly wait to read about Jacob for himself.

"You might have heard of the story where Jacob dreamed of a ladder ascending to heaven," Kim said. "The old spiritual 'We Are Climbing Jacob's Ladder' is based on that one. Jacob also wrestled with an angel one night and had his hip dislocated, leaving him with a permanent limp. His name means 'Deceiver,' which is pretty much the story of his life. His journey was one scheme after another until, believe it or not, God finally broke him loose. Jacob is going to help us learn to pray. You can think of this retreat as Outward Bound for the Soul."

Sam went through the rest of the session feeling unusually light-hearted, smiling readily and making a few notes in the journal that was provided for each participant. When they closed the evening with prayer and communion, he went to the table with gratitude. Only later did he realize that he hadn't worried about whether he was a poser, a problem he often had with communion. Clark assured him that everyone was welcome at the Lord's table, so he participated, but he wondered if Clark knew how uncertain he felt. Somehow Kim's words about Jacob seemed to take that fear away. He went out into the velvet evening with the taste of bread and wine still in his mouth.

Listening to the Text

The next morning Sam could hardly wait for the session to begin. Participants had been asked to refrain from unnecessary talking from 8 p.m. to 8 a.m., and Sam, normally reticent, needed to talk. He had gone back to his room after a short walk the night before and read the story of Jacob in his new Bible. What he discovered kept him awake well past midnight, his head spinning with questions and thoughts. It turned out that Jacob was far worse than Kim let on. He had slept with way more women than Sam ever had, and he was married to two sisters at the same time, even though he wasn't Mormon, and had babies with his wives' slave women—and it was his wives' idea! It was like a grade-B soap opera. And the whole thing was reported so matter-of-factly. This was the Word of God? What would Reverend

Family Values say about Jacob? And what were mandrakes? The story was so full of lies and women and goats he could hardly keep track. Jacob must have been totally trashed on his wedding night, not to realize the woman in his bed was someone other than his beloved Rachel.

Oh, yes, there was sweet little Rachel. Her conniving was so familiar. That's what Sam wrote in his journal. "She had Jacob wrapped around her little finger, and Jacob knew it, but he seemed powerless to do anything about it. He just kept trying to please her, trying to keep her happy. She was a little drama queen, pulling his chain. He never tried to trick Rachel, but with everyone else, watch out! What a con man. He and Laban deserved each other. Like Kim said, this guy had serious issues." Sam's feelings toward Jacob were complicated. Sam felt connected to him somehow, but was repulsed. How could a jerk like Jacob help anyone learn how to pray?

By the time Kim walked to the front and lit the candles, Sam and the others were seated. The wall of long windows revealed a beautiful, sunny morning, light filtering through the pine trees onto the altar at the front of the room. *This is more beautiful than any stained glass window*, Sam thought, watching the light dance through the trees.

"By now you've all read the story," Kim began, reaching for a dry-erase marker. She wrote two words on the board: *lectio divina*. "I asked you to read through it and pay attention to anything from the story that stood out to you, and to make a few notes about that in your journal. Would anyone like to volunteer something you noticed?"

There was a moment of silence, then Richard, a retired police officer, said, "These people obviously didn't have polygamy laws."

A titter of laughter was heard, then a young woman with short black hair, Michelle, spoke. "I thought Rachel was awesome. She lived in a man's world but she found a way to get what she wanted from life. She was fearless."

Without thinking, Sam blurted out, "Yeah, but look at how she treated the people around her. What's up with these sisters married to the same guy? My daughter is fourteen and I'm not sure I want her to read this." More laughter. Sam turned crimson at having spoken so quickly, cutting Michelle off, but others jumped in with their comments too. Sam was fascinated with how diverse their experiences were in reading the same story.

Kim obviously relished what was happening. "These people are so much like we are today. Anyone know a Rachel in your family or at work?" Heads nodded around the circle. "How about Laban, or Esau, or Jacob?" Everyone laughed and nodded. A few people muttered names under their breath.

"*Lectio divina* is the Latin name for sacred reading, the first form of prayer that we are going to learn about," Kim said. "What you did last evening, in reading Jacob's story, was the first step of *lectio*. You simply read the text without hurrying, paying attention to what is there." Kim went on to explain how this method of prayer opens people to the Bible so that it can read them. "God speaks to us through the text," she said. "We are all at different places in life and on our spiritual journeys. That's why we each noticed such different things about this story. It reads us according to where we are, what our questions are, what our issues are. You can read the same text again and again and different things will speak to you each time. This is why we call the Bible the living Word of God."

With deft skill Kim led the group through the remaining three steps of *lectio*. For each step she gave them time and space to practice listening. By the end of the morning Sam had, for the first time in his life, clearly heard God speak to him through the Bible about the details of his own life. It was as if Jacob's relationship with Rachel had performed open heart surgery on Sam, and a thorny, insidious tumor had been removed. He was beginning to understand why he had been so vulnerable to abusive women. God had shown him. *God* had shown him *in the Bible*. Sam took his lunch down by the lake, deeply grateful for the rule of silence at meals. He needed solitude.

Clarity

The group gathered for the next session to find a long piece of butcher paper taped to one wall. "Notice the pattern of choices in Jacob's life," Kim said, pointing to a large map she had drawn of Jacob's life. As she named each major crisis she taped a symbol for it onto the butcher paper, reminding the group of the whole story. "Each of these events was an opportunity for Jacob to become free of his false self and to come home to God. The false self is the collection of coping mechanisms and the masks we wear in order to gain approval of others, and to get what we want when we are wounded in life. The false self is something each of us develops. No one is exempt. In conflicts and crises we come face-to-face with our false self.

"Jacob was born into a life with unfair situations, the first being that his older brother would automatically inherit much more of the family treasure than Jacob would, not because he deserved it but because he happened to be born first. So you have Jacob from the very start of the story grasping Esau's heel. Jacob's story is archetypical for how we develop a false self in life, and how God works to set us free so that we can become our true selves."

Sam looked at the handout Kim had given them, with terms and definitions, finding "false self" and "archetype." He was beginning to see more clearly why he felt strangely connected to Jacob. But the talk about true and false self was a new concept and it sounded a little weird. It made him think of Luke Skywalker, but he wasn't about to say so to Kim.

Kim took a yellow marker and circled the places on the map where Jacob wrestled with the angel and then reconciled with Esau. "This is the turning point for Jacob," she noted. "He had to come to terms with his false self, with the way he schemed and deceived and took what belonged to others out of his own fears and jealousies, and maybe even his resistance against systems that automatically privileged some people and diminished others." Several women nodded their heads at the last comment. Michelle actually said, "Amen!"

Kim continued. "Jacob especially had to face how, with all of his mixed motives, he had really hurt his brother Esau. He had sinned against Esau. The angel gave him his new name, representing his true self, Israel. He would always limp after this episode, because he needed something to remind him of who he was, his real identity. His false self name was Deceiver. His true self name means 'One Who Struggles with God.'" Kim paused for a few minutes to allow people to ask questions.

Sam couldn't help remembering the sermons he had heard at the church after his first divorce. It was all so black and white about sin, and it just didn't seem true to his experience. It seemed to Sam that life was more complex than that. He wished the people in that other church could hear this teaching. It was so different.

Kim then opened a box and pulled out large sheets of manila paper. Handing one to each person, she said, "Okay, you learned how to read the Bible using *lectio divina*. Now we are going to use similar reading skills to look at our own lives. This is another form of contemplative prayer that requires listening and quiet, and paying attention. God speaks to us through our life events. On this paper we will make maps of our own life with its pattern of conflicts. Think of it as a Jacob map. Take plenty of time to do this. After you have completed your map, go back and slowly reflect on each event you put on the map. Your own story is the text. We are listening for God's invitation in our patterns of conflict and crisis. The invitation is to let go of the false self and say yes to our true selves, to become free and whole. It is unique for each of us. You don't have to share with anyone what comes to you. This is between you and God. You might find it helpful to make a few notes in your journal as you go along."

With that the group was dismissed for the rest of the afternoon, and Sam headed up the trail into the woods with his paper, journal, and pencil. An hour later he was staring at his map, unable to put into words what was happening inside. It was as if a city had been in a blackout and then the power came back on, one building at a time. Between reading the Jacob story with *lectio* and then making this map, Sam was able to trace a pattern of loneliness and grief that had caused him to make disastrous relationship choices, which then perpetuated more loneliness and grief. He could see where it got started, and where he was now. There was still a lot that was foggy, but he was beginning to come to clarity. He was starting to find answers to the questions he had asked Clark the day they went for coffee. And the answers were coming in prayer. Sam was praying.

It wasn't just that he was gaining clarity about his mistakes and failures. He could also see ways he had experienced kindness and love each time he had gone through a crisis. Bill, for example, had been there through the last divorce. God had always been there in people like Bill, and Sam hadn't even known it at the time. It was like Kim had said at one point, "goodness and mercy" really were following him "all the days of his life." Sam could scarcely take it in, that God's love had been reaching out to him throughout his life, and with such patience. The best news of all was that he wasn't doomed to keep repeating the same mistakes. If Jacob could change, so could he. "God, I am so thankful," he said, folding the map into his journal and walking back to the lodge. It didn't occur to him that he had just prayed out loud.

From Healing to Hospitality

The retreat was coming to a close. Sam had learned two more forms of contemplative prayer. One was called the prayer of examen, which involved a review at the end of the day, remembering moments that drew you into God's light and freedom and those that drew you away. Sam was so surprised at the lack of condemnation in these forms of prayer, even though they exposed his sin. There was a sense of acceptance of his own brokenness, along with receiving God's forgiveness and healing so that he could change.

The last method of prayer they learned about was the simplest of all. Kim called it "centering prayer." She used a verse from the Bible, "Be still, and know that I am God" (Ps. 46:10), to help them become quiet and focused, present to the love of God. Sam was especially taken with Kim's metaphor of swimming and floating in the mercy of God. He looked out the window and could see the sun sparkling off the surface of the lake. It seemed that no matter where he looked now, he saw images that took him back to something he had learned about prayer. Later, while swimming, he imagined himself floating in the presence of God. "Be still," he said to himself when his mind began to wander. "Know that I am God."

With each of these prayer examples Kim gave opportunities for everyone to practice and to connect it with the other two kinds of prayer they had learned. Each form of prayer had been powerful. It was hard for Sam to believe he had been gone only for the weekend. He felt like he had entered a new country, or had been given a new set of eyes. Everything seemed different now. He kept thinking about the people in his life. They were all Jacobs of some kind, just like he was. He smiled to himself, thinking about Kim's opening talk when she compared prayer to a wilderness journey. He hadn't had a clue then what she meant by climbing, resting, weeping, or going through the fog. But it was all making sense now. He could hardly wait to tell Jen about the retreat.

Kim was at the altar now, arranging several new objects. She draped a long, nubby piece of fabric over the surface and artfully arranged it so that it cascaded to the floor. The colors of the fabric mirrored the muted shades of the forest. Pieces of driftwood and pinecones were clustered at the center around three candles. The final touch was a plain glass pitcher full of water, which Kim had nestled in the pool of fabric at the base of the altar.

When the rest of the group had assembled, Kim touched the prayer bell to call the group to silent prayer, as they had learned to do the previous day. After five minutes she touched the bell again, its rich tone filling the beautiful space, echoing the newfound joy in Sam's heart.

"In our last session," Kim began, "we will look at the link between contemplative prayer, our own healing and integration, and the spiritual practice of hospitality. These three are inseparable. Hospitality means making a space for others, not so that we can exploit them or get something from them, or even so that we can make them be like us. It is showing them the same kind of grace and mercy, the same presence, that God has given us. As God shows us our own struggles and sins through God's eyes of mercy, we find healing for the wounds and liberation from the sins. We are able to change because the love of God is in us, helping us, bringing the pieces together. Knowing that God loves us in this way, that God is not ashamed of us, gives us a new perspective on ourselves and other people. The more we soak in that love from God, the more compassionate and hospitable we become to other people." She smiled at Sam then, a broad, affectionate smile. Sam ducked his head; he was pleased but felt bashful. He knew exactly what she meant. She was describing everything he had experienced at First Church.

"Sometimes people think contemplative prayer is self-centered and not action-oriented enough," Kim said. "This is because they do not understand its power to heal and transform us into the people God means for us to be. Contemplative prayer leads to the development of real holiness, so that our whole life is lived in God's light, the way God intended. The truth is, we become like the God we worship, the God who speaks to us in prayer. It turns out that contemplative prayer is the ground for all true intercession. It is a healing practice that takes us out into the world where we become good news."

Kim looked across the room and asked if anyone had any final questions before she offered the closing prayer. Carrie, another new-comer to First Church who worked at the county tax office, raised her hand. "How do you and the other pastors find time to practice contemplative prayer?" she asked. "You have jobs and families like we do. What is your secret?"

"We believe that prayer is the central responsibility and calling of the pastor," Kim answered, her face shining with passion and conviction. "Clark, Mike, Sylvia, and I are crazy enough to believe that if we prac-tice a rule of life together, with regular times for prayer in the morning and evening, and some other related spiritual disciplines, we will be the kind of pastors you deserve. We will have the love you deserve to receive from us, and we will hear from God what we should teach and preach so that you can be formed in your vocation as Christians. By commit-ting ourselves to prayer our church can be the kind of community God wants us to be in our city. So we make room in our schedule for prayer and shape the rest of the day around it. Sometimes it is hard, but we are very committed to this. We also agreed from the time we started the new old First Church that teaching the congregation to pray in the same way would be the first priority for preparing people for membership. If any of you are interested in becoming members of First Church in the future, this retreat that you have had is one of the requirements for preparation. We want everyone in ministry to do their ministry out of what they receive from God in prayer. We want everyone to live out of the central fact of God's love. That happens as we pray."

Afer the retreat, Sam nosed his car out of the parking lot onto the narrow road. Kim's final words about membership echoed in his mind. He hadn't heard a lot from the pastors about joining the church, another one of those little surprises. To hear Kim speak of prayer as the first preparation for membership was, well, unexpected. *He would have to find out more*, he thought as he began to whistle the tune to one of the songs they had sung at the retreat.

10

New Tongues of Fire

What we really need today are new tongues of fire, a new Pentecost in America. This alone will open us to the divine hospitality that is so radical that the walls of gender, race, and class dissolve in its healing reach. We need a Pentecostal outpouring that is about the love of God, a mighty wind that sweeps away the sinful caste systems that have deformed the American church. We need a baptism of cleansing fire that will heal the wounds of domestic violence and sexual abuse, that will liberate both the oppressed and the oppressor, that will send God's people out of the church into their neighborhoods with God's redeeming and reconciling love. It is time for the church to receive new languages, the kind that name, unmask, and engage the powers that are behind the threefold wound. This is the sanctifying force that called the Beguines into a life of kenotic love. It is the holy dynamism that led Julia Foote into her prophetic and evangelistic ministry in a church "deluded by a spirit of error." The untamed presence of the living God is the only power that can heal the threefold wound. Nothing else will do.

I am talking about a widespread surrender and obedience to God the Holy Spirit. Outside of North America, Pentecostalism is the fastest growing form of Christianity in the world. It is pan-denominational, and in many places it neither originated with nor resembles much of American Pentecostalism.[1] The Methodist Pentecostal Church, for instance, is the largest Pentecostal denomination in Chile. Among Chilean Methodist Pentecostals the emphasis is on the Holy Spirit's healing and empowerment of the church, rather than on speaking in tongues.[2] Chilean Methodist Pentecostals practice infant baptism and use a formal Methodist liturgy in their worship, practices that are not usually associated with Pentecostalism in North America.[3]

The kind of Pentecostalism needed in the United States is diametrically opposed to the hedonistic theology of much of contemporary American Pentecostalism. Here I am referring to prosperity gospel preachers with their multi-million-dollar empires. What we need is a Pentecostalism of the Lamb, a Spirit baptism that enables God's people to live the kenotic life. This Pentecostalism is open to all the gifts of the Spirit, to mystery and miracles, but those are not "the initial evidence." The evidence, initial and otherwise, is the healing of the threefold wound, the new kind of community. This is what Jesus was talking about when he said that there was one sign by which the world would know the gospel was true.[4] It is the one sign we most assiduously resist. The threefold wound has defined us for so long that we can scarcely imagine anything else. The wound seems "normal." We perpetuate it as the very will of God.

The new Pentecostalism would mean radical changes in how the church understands gender, race, and social location. There are countless ways in which these changes would impact the day-to-day life of

1. Allan Anderson, *An Introduction to Pentecostalism* (Cambridge: Cambridge University Press, 2004), 1.

2. Ibid., 13.

3. Because of the astonishing growth of Pentecostalism in the southern and eastern hemispheres, once-scorned Pentecostalism is now attracting a great deal of attention in the academy. For some recent studies, in addition to Anderson, see Amos Yong, *The Spirit Poured Out on All Flesh: Pentecostalism and the Possibility of Global Spirituality* (Grand Rapids: Baker Academic, 2005); Grant Wacker, *Heaven Below: Early Pentecostals and American Culture* (Cambridge: Harvard University Press, 2001); Harvey Cox, *Fire from Heaven: The Rise of Pentecostal Spirituality and the Reshaping of Religion for the 21st Century* (Cambridge, MA: Da Capo Press, 2001); and David Martin, *Tongues of Fire: The Explosion of Pentecostalism in Latin America* (Oxford: Blackwell, 1993).

4. John 17:20–26.

the church, but at the most basic level it would mean an egalitarian approach to leadership in the church, a preference for new church starts in disadvantaged urban and rural settings, and significant emphasis on ministries that prevent and heal the violence of the threefold wound.

An egalitarian approach to leadership in the church means that pastoral leadership would be carried out by teams whose ethnic and racial makeup is representative of the people in the neighborhood of the church. Women and men would share equally in power, service, and discernment. Rooted in a Pentecostal pneumatology, the church would actively resist in itself, and in the world at large, hierarchies of power based on distinctions of being "Jew or Greek, slave or free, male or female" (Gal. 3:28). Pastoral teams would be assembled to include a diversity of spiritual gifts so that the congregation could be equipped to the fullest extent possible. The pastors would understand their primary role as one of equipping the congregation in its missional vocation.

A preference for new church starts in forsaken urban and rural settings would mean that the church would live into the biblical narrative, taking the good news of Jesus to the crowded stables of Bethlehem instead of the opulent neighborhoods of the rich. The church would embrace a kenotic stance in relation to where and how it grows. Bivocational ministry by egalitarian teams of pastors would go a long way toward facilitating this model.

A missional vocation that focuses on the prevention and healing of violence caused by the threefold wound would mean that the church take seriously the facts of sexual abuse and domestic violence, which directly victimize a third of women and a sixth of men in the United States and indirectly wound everyone else.[5] The sinful ideology of sexism that drives violence against women is the deepest wound of all,

5. Statistically the figures vary slightly in different studies, but at this time about one out of three girls and one out of six boys in the United States is sexually abused before the age of eighteen. See FaithTrust Institute, "Q&A," www.faithtrustinstitute .org; Rape Victim Advocacy Program, "Myths and Facts—Child Sexual Abuse," www .rvap.org/pages/myths_and_facts_about_child_sexual_abuse; American Institute on Domestic Violence, "Domestic Violence in the Workplace Statistics," www.aidv-usa .com/Statistics.htm; and National Coalition against Domestic Violence, "Domestic Violence Facts," www.ncadv.org/files/domesticviolencefacts.pdf.

cutting across racial, ethnic, and economic lines, and in many ways undergirding racism and classism. The lack of real preparation for pastors to address these wounds cannot be overstated at this time.

It is possible to graduate from many, if not most, seminaries today without any substantive instruction in the facts of domestic violence or sexual abuse, the pervasive damage these sins inflict, the lifelong struggles with shame and other problems that result from such abuse, or how to provide pastoral care to survivors. While an elective class in these issues may be available, seminarians are generally not required to learn about the signs of abuse or strategies for intervention. These issues are simply not seen as primary to the preparation of pastors for ministry. How can it be that a course in Hebrew or church business administration can be required, but a class on the prevention and healing of violence is not, especially in light of the statistics? The very prioritization of courses for people seeking a master's of divinity degree reflects the numbing pervasiveness of the threefold wound.

The church in the night is like Lazarus, awaiting the Lord's command to come forth from the tomb. The voice of Jesus calls even now to roll away the stone, to unbind the body of Christ, to release the church to its true vocation. This is what the new Pentecost will do. It will resurrect the church, and what a glorious church that will be.

Returning to our narrative of Sam, who is being evangelized in a community shaped by the new Pentecostalism, we will see how one of the pastors, Sylvia, experienced the healing of the threefold wound in her own life. We can then see how her healing led to some of the primary ministries of First Church in its neighborhood. While this story represents one possible configuration for egalitarian leadership teams and the other features of the new Pentecostalism, there are many other possible models.

Samaritan Women

Sam crawled out from under the table, having plugged in another power strip for Sylvia's display. The block party would start soon. Everything needed to be ready. Sam had offered to help with whatever he could, so Sylvia had nabbed him to assist with her display on the battered women's shelter and the recovery groups. Every fall First Church threw a block party, which was really a misnomer, because after the first year more and more people came to it from the wider neighborhood. It was a festive event with plenty of good food and games for the kids. Local musicians offered their talents for entertainment. There were tables and booths with information about the church's ministries, along with information about other community churches, agencies, and groups. The idea was to get everyone together who had a stake in the well-being of the neighborhood, show hospitality, and let the people see the healing emphases of the church.

Sam watched Sylvia as she took out bundles of leaflets and bookmarks. Her three children played tag nearby, dashing in and out of tables and boxes. "Marcos, I said not to go over there where they're cooking!" she shouted. Marcos trotted back, his black curls and large brown eyes a miniature version of his mother's. "Sam, you want some more kids? You only have one. That's not enough. Take Marcos home, okay?" Marcos, a complete extrovert, threw his arms around Sam. His little round face peered up at Sam playfully. "Yes, take me home. *Pleeeease*. I need to get away from my sisters!" Just then Rosa darted in, tapping Marcos and speeding away. "You're it!" They ran shrieking toward the church lawn where some women were setting up a ring game for the kids.

After the display was finished Sylvia reached for a thermos and poured two steaming cups of coffee, giving one to Sam. "I really appreciate your help with my display," she said. "The block party is always so much fun. It's a great way to meet people who are new in the neighborhood."

"Well, I have to admit I have mixed motives in helping you," Sam confessed, smiling his lopsided grin. "I'm curious about how you got involved working at the shelter. You're passionate about justice, but you're so, I don't know, good-natured about everything. I guess you've ruined my stereotypes about scary activists." Sylvia laughed and tried to make a scary face, but it didn't work.

Sam continued. "How did you get started at the shelter? Was it because of First Church? And I know you are in seminary and was wondering how you keep all the balls in the air with your job and family and everything."

"You are full of questions!" she said with a chuckle. Propping her feet up on a box, Sylvia gestured around at the people working at the booths and beginning to trickle into the street. "Look at all these people, Sam. Every one of them has a story. One of every three women walking past us has been sexually abused as a child. For men it's one in six."

"I had no idea!" Sam gasped, taken aback by the numbers.

"It gets worse," Sylvia said. "Domestic violence is the number-one cause of injury to women in America. The number-one cause of death to American women in the workplace is homicide, and most of the time the perpetrator is the woman's intimate partner. These things are true whether the woman is rich or poor, educated or illiterate, and regardless of race. It happens in every social, religious, and economic class. And the most pitiful thing about it is that historically the church has only made matters worse." Sylvia turned sideways a little to look at Sam, trying to decide how much to say.

"Most churches I've been to, which admittedly are very few, seem not to talk about those issues," Sam said. "I don't think I've ever heard a sermon about domestic violence or sexual abuse. I have heard a lot of comments from the pulpit about sexual sin, but not sexual abuse." He was quiet for a moment. "That's kind of weird when you think about it. Sexual abuse is the worst kind of sexual sin, I would say."

"Yes, that's *exactly* how I feel," Sylvia said. "Most of the sermons I heard about sexual sin, back before First Church, focused on the sin of sex outside of marriage. Pastors completely ignored the fact of sexual abuse and how it affects people. I never heard any sermons on the shame that comes from sexual abuse, or the fact that many women are raped and in other ways sexually abused in marriages by their husbands. It was like, if you're married, anything goes. If you were married your husband could do to you things he would go to jail for if he did them to anyone else. I never heard anyone talk about these things at church. That's what got me started. I went and got a new study Bible and started reading the Gospels to see if Jesus said anything about this stuff. That was when I first began to attend worship here at First Church. I knew Kim just a little bit, but not Clark."

"Were you shocked when you read it?" Sam asked. "I read about Jacob at Kim's prayer retreat and it blew my mind. I couldn't believe those stories were in the Bible. They seemed so, well, adult. But that story of Jacob changed my life."

Sylvia laughed, her face alive with joy and freedom. "I know what you mean. Yes, I was surprised, Sam, especially when I read the story of the woman at the well in John 4. I felt I was reading a story about myself. I finally came to Christ by reading that story."

"So, tell me the story," Sam said. "I don't know that one yet."

"Well, you know the disciples were all learning disabled, right?" she began. Sam chuckled. He had indeed picked up on that issue.

"Okay, so one day Jesus and his disciples were on their way some-where and they stopped at this well to rest. Jesus sent them on to get lunch in town and he stayed behind. I think he wanted to get them out of his hair. It was the middle of the day and Jesus was hot and tired and really thirsty. This woman came from town to the well to draw water. She was all by herself. Jesus asked her for a drink."

"Seems reasonable enough," Sam said.

"Actually, it was scandalous because Jewish men didn't mix with women in public because of purity laws."

"What? You've got to be kidding," Sam said, appalled.

"I know, it seems strange to us, but that's the way it was," Sylvia said. "And there were a lot of other outrageous things about this encounter. The woman was a Samaritan on top of being a woman. The Samaritans were despised by the Jews, who viewed them as pretty much subhuman for religious and racial reasons. Plus, she was at the well when all the other women were at home, which means she probably had moral issues and was being ostracized by the other women. The well was where the women got together every day to talk to their friends, catch up on news, give each other advice. Not this woman; she drew water by herself. So she was an outcast among her own people too."

"Wow," Sam said. "And Jesus talked to her?"

"Yes, about all sorts of things, especially theology."

"Theology?"

"Yes, that was part of what made this so unusual. In Jesus's day men didn't think women could do theology. I guess some people think that today too." Sylvia smiled mischievously. "But here Jesus was, talking to this woman as if she was equal to anyone. The thing is,

Jesus grew up in a culture with taboos against even being in the same space with a Samaritan, much less asking to drink from a Samaritan woman's cup. Can you imagine? Jesus was breaking through walls of gender, race, religion, and class—pretty much every major taboo of his culture. It was really scandalous. But I'm getting ahead of myself. This woman asked Jesus how he could ask to drink from her jar when she was a Samaritan and he was a Jew.

"Jesus started telling her about how he had living water for her," Sylvia said. "That was all it took. She had so many questions about worship and the Messiah. It was like she had been waiting forever to have someone to ask all these spiritual questions. Maybe she was a woman, maybe she was a Samaritan, maybe she had issues, but still, she was just like anyone else, wondering about God and what life meant. All of a sudden Jesus told her to go call her husband, knowing full well that she had been married and divorced five times and was now living with a partner."

"Five times? Five?" Sam said. "Why didn't anyone ever tell me the Bible was like this? I would have read it a long time ago."

Sylvia nodded, eager to continue. "Well, by that time the woman realized Jesus was at least a prophet, and maybe more than a prophet. Jesus finally told her he was indeed the Messiah that both the Jews and Samaritans had been waiting for. Just then the disciples showed up with their lunch and they were shocked to see Jesus talking with this woman and breaking all these taboos. They didn't know what to say. The woman ran back to town and told everyone that she had met a man who knew everything about her, and could this be the Messiah, and they had better come and meet him. As a result of what she said many people became Christians in that town."

"This is a great story," Sam said. "You said it helped you become a Christian. Was it because Jesus treated the woman like a normal person? I mean, in light of everything you said about taboos, that would have been mind-boggling for her."

Sylvia paused, studying Sam and wondering how much to share. "The thing is, Sam, I talked to Kim about this story because I felt like that woman, outcast by my people and the religious community from my childhood because of my divorce. When I saw that Jesus loved the woman and had faith in her ability to think about theology, and when I realized that she actually evangelized her town, it opened my eyes to new ways of thinking about my own journey."

Sam nodded, marveling at the way stories in the Bible could bring insight and healing to hurts that were almost too painful to name. He thought about Kim again, and the way she knew just which stories from the Bible to give to people to help them.

Sylvia continued. "Kim told me that the woman at the well was probably a survivor of abuse, because she wouldn't have had the right to divorce those husbands, and all the signs in her story point to someone who had been passed around and used most of her life. This would be one reason she was at the well by herself in the heat of the day, when she wouldn't have to endure the looks and comments from the other women in town. Kim said Jesus saw through the woman's sin and failures to the hurts that drove her life. He saw her goodness and worth, her potential. Jesus picked her to be the first evangelist to the Samaritans. He did it to let her know how much he loved her, and to teach the disciples about the sinfulness of racism, sexism, and other kinds of bigotry." Sylvia's voice had become quietly intense. As Sam looked into her eyes he saw scars and haunting memories. Most of all, he saw courage.

"That's what really did it, Sam, when Kim told me about this woman as a survivor of abuse. She became my hero. How could I not love and trust Jesus after what he did for her? I myself am a survivor of childhood abuse and adult domestic violence. I nearly left the Christian faith because of all the shaming and destructive messages I was given from the pulpit and otherwise. When I needed someone to believe me and to help me, what I got was blame, as if the abuse was my fault, and instructions to go back and submit to my husband because if I was meek and quiet maybe my husband would get saved."

Sam's reaction was visceral. "Wait a minute," he said. "You mean to tell me the church blamed you for the violence you suffered?" He began to feel angry in a way he had not allowed himself to feel in a very long time. "How could they blame you? What the hell were they thinking?"

"I know what you mean, Sam. Their logic was messed up. It had to do with their interpretation of the Bible. They thought I was wrong, on every count. I was a problem because I was a woman, and a Latina at that. I was wrong in complaining about my husband since he was the breadwinner and what they called the spiritual head of our house, even though I was the only one who went to church or prayed or tried to help our daughter learn about God. I was wrong because I wasn't being submissive to my husband in his abuse. They didn't look at it as a situation of injustice or breaking the law. It never occurred to them how the violence was impacting my daughter and her future."

"Well what did you do?" Sam asked, leaning forward. He hadn't suffered nearly the amount of violence Sylvia had, but his own experience of being shamed and labeled gave him deep sympathy for what she had been through.

"I left my husband," Sylvia said, firmly and quietly. "I took Teresa and what clothes and food and other things we could fit into our old car, and we drove away one night after he had fallen asleep. I went to a battered women's shelter in another city and asked for help. I was too terrified to go to the one in my community. My husband had threatened to kill me if I ever tried to leave him, and I believed him. I found out later that most women who are killed by their partners die while they are trying to leave the abusive relationship. At the shelter they took me in and helped me get my life together. I needed to move and to get a different job, and I needed to get a restraining order and so many other scary things I had never done. Each one of them seemed insurmountable. But the women at the shelter helped me."

"Thank God for that!" Sam paused. "So then what happened? You are now working at the shelter, so they must have seen great potential in you."

"Actually, I'm not at that shelter." Sylvia turned toward him, energetic again, the familiar spark of mischief in her voice. "I started the shelter where I work now. We needed one in this part of town. I would not have believed it possible for me to do such a bold thing as to start a battered women's shelter ten years ago. I was so diminished by the abuse, the constant belittling and threats, the names, the control. But I learned first from Kim and then Clark, and through my own times of prayer and reading the Bible, that the power of the Holy Spirit can heal any wound. I have experienced so much healing from God. I have told you just a small part of it. I still can't believe it sometimes, that God would call me into ministry, but it is true. I am doing exactly what God called me to do." Sylvia turned toward Sam, throwing her hands up in amazement. "Can you believe it?" she asked. "Isn't God great?"

Sam nodded his head silently and seemed to be on the verge of saying something, but unable to find the words.

Aware of his struggle, Sylvia stood up and motioned for Sam to follow. "You know what, Sam? I'm kind of hungry. Maybe we should go get some of those hamburgers."

As they walked across the street Sam finally spoke. "Sylvia, what you have been through and where you are now, it's nothing short of miraculous. Your story touches something very deep in me." Sam paused, searching for the courage for the next few words. "And I just wanted to say I know what it's like to be with an abusive spouse." Sam could scarcely say the words, but he needed to name the reality of his own suffering. As he spoke he felt the familiar wave of shame that arose whenever he remembered the fights, the accusations, and cruel words. In some complicated way that he was only beginning to understand, the humiliation was linked to his gender as well as the abuse. Because of these feelings Sam never had allowed himself to use the word "abuse" to describe what he had endured, nor had he allowed himself to think very long about the reason for this reluctance. But this time he felt something else alongside the shame, something new and fragile, but very real. What Sam felt was the beginning of his own liberation.

Sylvia looked into Sam's eyes for a long moment. "I could sense that, Sam, that you knew something about abuse," she said. "I had a feeling you've been down some hard roads. It shows in your compassion."

11

Your Will Be Done on Earth

Could it be that we have missed the most basic meaning of Jesus's words, "your will be done, *on earth*" (Matt. 6:10)? For what could be more clear than God's will for the earth and its creatures, human and otherwise, to experience shalom? Yet how often have we prayed the Lord's Prayer without any thought for the ecosystems of this earth?

As Bonaventure and Woolman demonstrate so well, the earth belongs to God who created it and pronounced it "good." Genesis 1–3 teaches us that the first way humanity experiences God is through the goodness of creation, the concrete realities of air, food, water, and shelter, the abundant forms of life. The universal evangelistic witness given to all people everywhere, Paul tells us, is creation pointing to the God who is there.[1] When the church ignores, exploits, or damages creation, it hinders one of the most important and universal means God has chosen to lead people to know and love the Creator. By neglecting or resisting creation care, the church becomes a stumbling block to the witness of creation. By practicing creation care, the church contributes to the fullest possible witness to the reality of a good and loving God.

1. Rom. 1:20.

But there is more to the sanctity of creation, Bonaventure tells us. God is most fully revealed to the world as the Potter becomes the clay. In the incarnation Christ hallows for all time the common dust of this earth and all its creatures.[2] Through the power of the risen Christ the church has the ability to mediate the healing of a sin-disordered natural world. Eco-evangelism is committed to the missional vocation of honoring and working for the healing of God's good earth, in the name and Spirit of Christ.

With today's mushrooming environmental crises, the church has unprecedented responsibility to practice eco-evangelism, an essential element of a contemplative stance. The church is charged with speaking, being, and doing good news to the earth and all its creatures.

Three Practices

The church can and should practice eco-evangelism in three basic ways. First, the church can return to a theology of stewardship that is not primarily about money but about our relationship with God's earth and its creatures. Second, the church as a community can practice and promote creation care through its use of resources and its participation in creation care in the local community. It should do this corporately and as individuals and families. Third, the church can and must take a prophetic stance against unchecked consumerism, the materialistic god of this age that devours and poisons people, animals, forests, and water, leaving desolate wastelands in its wake. We can be certain that when the church practices eco-evangelism in these three ways, in conjunction with attending to the threefold wound as described previously, it will gain the moral authority it requires if it is to speak convincingly of the gospel to our bruised and broken world.

The shift to a theology of stewardship grounded in creation care rather than money will not come easily to the American church. We have been so indoctrinated to think of stewardship in terms of finance campaigns and tithing that any other form of stewardship seems secondary. Most church members know that when pastors speak of

2. David Baker and Elaine Heath, *More Light on the Path* (Grand Rapids: Baker Academic, 1999), 14.

stewardship they include the words "time, talent, and treasure" or something similar, but what they really mean is financial giving. The annual stewardship campaign is always focused on money.

A theology of stewardship that is focused on creation care does not sidestep the question of stewarding financial resources, but money is not the primary concern. The model that I am recommending is much more challenging and subversive than merely asking people to tithe. It is more than possible, for example, for Christians to tithe and at the same time blithely participate in rampant consumerism and the exploitation of earth's limited resources. The model of stewardship that I am advancing takes into account John Woolman's wisdom and practice. The use of natural resources is measured in light of the cost to people, animals, and the earth, not just locally but globally. The accumulation of needless luxuries is seen in light of its devastation of the earth, animals, and people, and the sinful accumulation of wealth for the few at great cost to the laboring poor. The ramifications of this theology of stewardship are much greater than simply giving 10 percent of one's income. The practice of giving one's money to mission is just one part of a much larger lifestyle of kenosis.

To put it very simply, this theology of stewardship is grounded in the conviction that the Christian lifestyle, in regard to material goods, should be one of simplicity, adequacy, and sustainability. To live otherwise is to dishonor the God we claim to love.

Promoting creation care in the church begins with the old adage, "reduce, reuse, recycle." Churches should do everything possible to facilitate these practices in the church's collective stewardship of material resources and in the lives of individual members. One of the obvious places to begin is in the buildings churches use. Much is to be said for networks of house churches that meet on Sunday in a local school auditorium, especially when the school is "green." The practice of building and owning ever-larger campuses with massive auditoriums to accommodate larger and larger crowds should be questioned in light of the costs to the environment. Is it really necessary to have churches the size of football stadiums? How does this practice lead to the healing of a wounded earth and to the formation of disciples who practice a lifestyle of kenosis?

Imagine the testimony to a watching world if the church decided to practice simplicity and adequacy in its ownership and use of property and material goods. What if churches cooperatively shared property and buildings to maximize the use of an existing building instead of building more and more structures that require heating and air-conditioning for people who come for a few hours each week? What if the church did this explicitly to contribute to a cleaner, healthier world out of evangelistic love of neighbor?

This worldview would lead to core values that are notably lacking in much of the American church. Among these would be a commitment to simpler lifestyles. Church members would learn as part of stewardship education that public transportation, bicycles, and walking are to be preferred over private automobiles whenever possible, that food grown locally is more environmentally friendly than food imported from across the globe, that tap water is healthier for the environment, our pocketbooks, and our bodies than is expensive bottled water. Quarterly or monthly clean-up days would be part of the church's mission, with congregants working to remove litter from neighborhood beaches, roadsides, and parks as part of creation care. The church would participate actively in recycling programs, and if such programs are not available in a community the church would be the first to initiate the formation of such programs. These are just a few of the ways eco-evangelism could be practiced as part of a contemplative stance. They are all grounded in the conviction that stewardship is above all else about our relationship to God's earth and its creatures.

As Woolman made so clear, it is the Christian vocation to actively resist the exploitation and destruction of God's earth and the powers and principalities that drive the devastation. This means a sharp critique and resistance to unchecked consumerism and the commodification of science and technology. From the smallest resistance to nonbiodegradable plastic bags, to resistance to recreational shopping, to activism against strip mines in West Virginia, Christians should be at the forefront of resistance to the degradation of the earth. This is part of our evangelistic task, part of a contemplative stance.

As we have seen thus far in the narrative of Sam and his newfound friends, alternative forms of church really are possible in postmodern

America. Not only are they possible, they are deeply attractive. As
Sam is about to discover, when the church practices eco-evangelism
as part of its ethos of kenosis, the outcome is transformation.

Oakwood Creek

Sam made the last turn onto Braxton Street, driving slowly so that he
could find Mike and Libby's house, the yellow one with white shutters
and a big porch swing. The street was in a shabby old neighborhood
with chain link fences and plastic statues of the Blessed Virgin. Cars
spilled from driveways into the front yards. Overhead the power lines
crisscrossed into a thousand rectangles, dissecting the leaden sky.
Dogs seemed to be in every yard, most of them wildly announcing
Sam's presence. Leaves scuttled down the street, driven by the brisk
November wind. Sam walked up to the front porch and found the
doorbell nearly hidden behind corn stalks, pumpkins, and gourds.
Paper cutouts of pilgrims, turkeys, and cornucopias filled the living
room window. Sam could tell Libby was a third-grade teacher. The
porch exuded a message of welcome and safety, of good things to eat
and games to play, of family.

Almost before Sam pressed the button the door flew open, allowing a rush of warm, cookie-scented air to escape. Inside was laughter
and music. Mike and Libby's two daughters, Katy and Beth, were in
the kitchen with several friends baking sugar cookies. Sam could see
the kitchen was a glorious mess. Katy squealed when she saw Sam
and ran to him with a misshapen turkey cookie. "You have to eat
this. I made it!"

Sam stuffed the whole cookie in his mouth, rubbing his belly and
smiling happily. "Turkey! My favorite, but where's the gravy?"

Mike sent Katy back to the kitchen and gestured toward the den.
"Come on, Sam, it's a little less noisy in here. Not much, but a little."
Sam noticed the family photos on the walls and the comfortable old
furniture. The feeling of peace was palpable.

"We'll be meeting at the park in about a half hour," Mike said.
"I think there will be five or six of us this time. I have garbage bags

and rakes in the garage. Do you have gloves? You'll need them. Hey, thanks for coming to help with the cleanup."

Sam grinned in response. "Believe me I'm glad to be involved. Ever since Bill told me about your decision to move to this neighborhood I've wanted to know more about it. You've really inspired him, you know. I think he may do something similar."

"Well, it was a family decision," Mike said. "Libby and I talked about it for a long time, over a period of a few months actually. It's not a decision to make quickly. Living on less can sound romantic but it's a challenge. Sometimes it's hard, especially when the kids ask for luxuries we could probably afford if we poured all our resources just into our own family. We have to think this through on a regular basis. All the same, it has been liberating for us. And I can't begin to tell you how much joy it has given us to really get to know our neighbors and be a part of this neighborhood. There are some great people living here. They're a blessing to us."

"Well, I have to say I never met anyone who did downward mobility on purpose," Sam said with a laugh. "It's pretty radical. I don't think I could do it. Maybe someday though."

Mike held up a lumpy looking ceramic bowl that had been sitting on the coffee table. The artist had attempted to glaze it with a camouflage look, but the result was more like charred wood. "One of the kids down the street made this for me at school," he said, beaming. "Kevin's dad abandoned the family when he was a baby, so he's never even met his own dad. His mom works two jobs and can just barely make ends meet. They're good people but life is hard for them. Kevin is like my own nephew now. Look at this. I feel rich every time I look at this bowl. Libby and I don't think of living here as a sacrifice. It's just the right thing for us to do. Who knows what kind of opportunities Kevin will have as an adult? He'll have grown up in a neighborhood where he has the equivalent of an extended family looking out for him, and if all goes as well as we hope, he'll get a college education. Kevin and his mom know we believe in them."

Sam took the bowl and looked at the bottom, where Kevin had written in uneven, childish script, "To my frind Mike." He thought about Jen and the many opportunities she had for extracurricular activities, band trips, sports, and music. Despite her parents' divorce she still knew that both parents loved her and would be there for her as she grew up.

"What is the hardest thing about the changes you made in moving here?" Sam asked, positioning the bowl carefully back in the center of the table.

Mike pondered for a moment before answering. "Well, at first it was hard to give up some of the luxuries we had come to think of as needs. Eating out three or four times a week was one of them. We downsized from three cars to one, and started using public transportation as much as possible. That was annoying at first, especially when we were in a hurry. But we gradually got used to it and began to see that we didn't need to jump in the car and drive somewhere every time we felt like it. The decreased number of trips to the mall were an adjustment, too. We didn't realize until we committed to living on less just how often we had engaged in recreational shopping. I think the hard part was owning just how materialistic we had been. It was humbling."

"But what about living in a higher-crime neighborhood? Did that worry you, especially with having children?" Sam could see that Mike and Libby worked hard to create a home that is a haven not just for their own family, but for everyone who came to visit. They were utterly hospitable.

"Naturally we wanted the kids to be safe," Mike said. "Believe it or not, the crime rate in this neighborhood is actually lower than in some of the affluent parts of the city. And by being involved in our neighborhood we are helping this to be a safer place to live for ourselves and everyone else in the community. The more you build community, the safer a community is. It's more about neighbors knowing each other and being on good terms than how affluent a neighborhood is." Mike glanced at his watch and stood up. "It's about time to head down to the park. Maybe the girls will let us steal a few of their cookies."

Ten minutes later they were at Oakwood Creek, a long, narrow, green space with playground equipment that had seen better days. A stream flowed along one side, its banks littered with trash that had washed up during the last storm. As Mike and Sam opened the trunk of the car and put on their work gloves, several other people arrived to help. They were all from the neighborhood, people Mike and Libby had gradually befriended. Before long Sam felt as if he had known all of them for years. As they worked together, laughing and talking, the work of cleaning the park was actually fun.

By the end of the afternoon the last beer can and plastic bag had been picked up and sorted so that as much as possible could be recycled. Sam looked around the park with satisfaction. He had always loved the outdoors but had never paid much attention to small city parks like this one. He never felt he was really outdoors until he left the city completely, which he did as often as possible. But working with Mike and the others had given him a different perspective. A small green space like this one might be the only "great outdoors" some people would ever have, and taking good care of it could help them experience the beauty of nature they otherwise would miss. A flock of geese flew overhead, their graceful silhouettes moving against the scudding clouds.

Sam mentioned to Mike how he originally noticed that First Church was green when he saw the recycling bins in the fellowship hall. Mike told him how he and the other pastors decided to teach stewardship as creation care. They believed that if people understood and embraced respect for God's earth and the wise use of its resources, if they practiced sustainability as much as possible, that would be the foundation for a healthy relationship to money and material possessions. Mike mentioned the first three chapters of Genesis as their foundational text for understanding stewardship. Sam had never heard it explained this way, but it made so much sense.

When Sam and Mike got back to the house the sun was low in the sky. Libby urged Sam to stay for dinner, but he declined. He needed to take care of some things at home, he said, thanking Mike again for inviting him to help with the park project. What he really needed to do was think.

Baptismal Water

As Sam left the neighborhood and turned toward home, he couldn't help but marvel at how different his life was now. He had been part of First Church for a little over a year, gradually getting to know more people, eventually taking part in several outreach ministries. Throughout this time no one had ever pressured him to change, to join the church, or to do anything. Yet the very openness and hospitality made Sam want to come back, made him want to open himself to the gospel they proclaimed.

When he got home Sam went to his desk and took out the pictures from the prayer retreat. He reached for the prayer journal Kim had given him, and his Bible, which by now was beginning to feel like a trusted friend. Settling into his favorite chair, Sam slowly looked through all the pictures, savoring the memories of the conversations, hikes, and times of worship. Selecting one of the photos, a close-up of the altar arrangement on the last day, Sam placed it on the coffee table. He opened his Bible to the story of Jacob, recalling with an unexpected surge of emotion how transforming it had been to read that story and hear it speak to his own life, setting in motion a series of events that were liberating and healing. Sam placed the open Bible on the table next to the picture. Then he took the journal, which was still mostly empty, but which contained reflections Sam had written at the retreat and other times as he had come to deeper levels of understanding about his life and what it meant to have faith. He recalled his conversations with Clark, Sylvia, and Mike. He thought about the beauty of the shabby little park after the litter had all been removed. He remembered the love that bound Mike, Libby, and their family to their neighbors in Oakwood.

Holding the journal in both hands, Sam began to weep. He could no longer contain the gratitude and joy, the freedom, the hope that welled up from deep within. He was a new man, a changed man, a man who had come home to God and to himself. Sam laughed and cried, rocking back and forth, thanking God over and over for leading him into the light. He thanked God for Bill, for Clark, for Kim and Sylvia and Mike, for every one of the homeless people who came to worship at First Church, and for the shabby old building that was a hospital for so many wounded souls. He thanked God for Jen and for all the people in his life, for the incredible gift of relationships. Sam wept his wordless prayer, offering himself to God to be a blessing to others, just as others had been a blessing to him. After a long time he grew quiet again, spent with the experience. He put the journal beside the Bible and the picture. Outside the rain began to fall, the first light drops quickly changing to a torrent. Reaching for the telephone, Sam dialed Clark's number.

Sam didn't realize until Clark answered the phone in a sleepy voice that it was far too late to call. Clark was kind, as always. "Hi Sam. It's kind of late. Are you okay?"

"Yes, I'm fine, more than fine." Sam's words tumbled out, a disjointed stream of joy and gratitude. "I know what it means now. First Church has shown me, you have shown me, all of you, what it means to believe in Jesus and follow him. I finally get it! Being a Christian isn't about rules and never having made wrong choices. It's a whole crazy way of life, crazy in a good way. It's receiving mercy, giving yourself away for others, finding peace and healing in the process. I can't get over it, how much God loves us, and how uncomplicated it is. Clark, I just had to tell you, I want to be baptized. I am a Christian."

Epilogue

Out of the Night

I emerge from the tomb of my slumber
Loose the attachments
That bound me for so long
No one guessed at my beauty

I leave the stifling night of my confinement
Slide into the cool baptismal waters
Suspended in the breaking of the dawn
Stroke on stroke
Stroke on stroke
I glide
Suspended in mercy

Now I emerge
Now I breathe
Now I sing
Now I live

Your redemption

Appendix

Corporate Experiences of the Dark Night

Some readers, no doubt, will object to my use of the classic threefold contemplative path to describe what is happening in the American church.[1] To apply the path to a corporate body, much less to the church, some will argue, is to misread the great mystics, and to generalize too broadly a conceptual framework meant only for individuals. Some readers may particularly object to my hermeneutic of the dark night of the soul as a purgative process that encompasses the church and not just individuals on their journey. This objection is understandable.

---

1. The threefold conceptual framework has its origin scripturally in Eph. 4:11–24. Readers are exhorted to die to the old self and "put on Christ," putting away all that is of the old life and its ego-driven concerns. Patristic theologians, beginning with Origen (185–254) and culminating in Evagrius Ponticus (346–399), laid the groundwork for the articulation of the three ways. Pseudo-Dionysius (ca. 500) labeled the three stages as purgation, illumination, and union. The concept of a threefold path for spiritual advancement received further, somewhat more lyrical explication at the hands of the mystics Bernard of Clairvaux (1090–1153) and Catherine of Siena (1347–1380). By the time of the Quietist controversy in the seventeenth century, "the three ways" had become so foundational to Roman Catholic spirituality that Miguel de Molinos, one of the proponents of Quietism, was pronounced a heretic partly because of his rejection of the three ways as a norm for spiritual advancement (Thomas D. McGonigle, "Three Ways," in *The New Dictionary of Catholic Spirituality*, ed. Michael Downey [Collegeville, MN: Liturgical Press, 1993], 963–65).

In the history of Western Christian theology the development of language about apophatic spirituality has been oriented toward the individual spiritual journey so that even those who specialize in contemplative or spiritual theology may hesitate to think in terms of a corporate experience of the threefold path. The late Gerald May, for example, senior fellow of contemplative theology and psychology at the Shalem Institute, noted that social systems including marriages, families, institutions, and nations seem to experience something of a dark night, but he was hesitant to "over-anthropomorphize social systems," thus remaining cautious when considering the possibility of a corporate dark night of the soul.[2] He found the idea deeply attractive but difficult to map.

May's caution is wise, serving as a warning that it is easy to read spiritual texts (canonical and noncanonical) anachronistically, and with the best of intentions do violence to those texts, importing an agenda that co-opts their power. Frankly, this is a danger any time we pray with the Bible, for example, reading the Scriptures by means of *lectio divina*.[3] To open ourselves to the possibility of the text speaking to us in new ways is to surrender a certain measure of control, thus at times Christians have indeed "heard" a text say something that leads not to life but to death. This is why such readings should be done in the context of Christian community, with the wisdom of the sages (living and dead) to help guide and shape our hermeneutic.

The communal nature of faith that is deeply rooted in the Bible and that has been so marginalized in the Western church, as well as the ecclesiastical terrain of the contemporary American church, compel me toward a corporate understanding. To be sure, the dark night is always obscure, thus any "diagnosis" of the night in a communal sense must be bracketed with the awareness that only God knows with certainty if a dark night is what is taking place. All discussion of the dark night, along with any other aspect of the spiritual journey, must be done with humility and the continual awareness that we "see

2. May, *Dark Night of the Soul*, 176.

3. *Lectio divina* is the ancient practice of praying the Scriptures using four steps: reading, meditating, praying, and contemplating. For an excellent introduction to the history and practice of *lectio divina* see Thelma Hall, *Too Deep for Words* (Mahwah, NJ: Paulist Press, 1988).

through a glass darkly." Thus to such critics I offer both appreciation for their desire to preserve the integrity of the traditional understanding of the dark night and an invitation to consider a more generous reading of the mystical texts. The writings of John of the Cross, Teresa of Avila, Ignatius of Loyola, Madame Guyon, and others can and should be read as a holy matrix through which to understand our own experiences of darkness and loss, of the seeming withdrawal of God and other aspects of the night.[4] Paul Ricoeur's hermeneutical method of the "second naïveté" serves well not only for Scripture but also for spiritual texts such as these.[5]

Others may challenge the theological concept of a *divinely initiated* dark night, claiming that the classic articulation of the dark night of the soul is simply a premodern way to describe clinical depression or some other psychological malady. Out of a struggle with questions of theodicy, some may resist the idea that God would initiate any process that leads individuals or groups to experience suffering of any kind. Georgia Harkness, for example, describes the dark night as "fundamentally an anxiety neurosis," a "sin and a sickness," and never the direct will of God.[6] Unquestionably some cases of depression, anxiety disorders, and so on have been mislabeled a "dark night," adding to the already heavy burden of those who suffer. Sometimes the experience of the dark night includes clinical depression, anxiety, grief, or some other painful challenge. At times the night is precipitated by an experience of loss, such as the death of a loved one.[7] Yet the dark night and depression are not the same. John of the Cross himself makes distinctions between "melancholia" and the dark night.[8] Denys Turner comments that the dark night is, rather, a "dialectical critique

4. Mark McIntosh (*Mystical Theology*, 135) provides a well-reasoned apologetic for this approach to mystical texts, specifically in reference to the spiritual exercises of St. Ignatius.

5. Mark I. Wallace explores the second naïveté in Ricoeur's hermeneutic of Scripture, yet the same hermeneutical method can be used fruitfully with noncanonical mystical texts (*The Second Naiveté: Barth, Ricoeur, and the New Yale Theology*, 2nd ed. [Macon, GA: Mercer University Press, 1995], xi–xv).

6. Georgia Harkness, *The Dark Night of the Soul* (Nashville: Abingdon, 1945), 71, 111.

7. For more on the uniqueness of the night for different individuals, see Underhill, *Mysticism*.

8. John of the Cross, *Dark Night of the Soul*, Book 1, chapter 9.2.

of experientialist tendencies."⁹ May offers extensive commentary on
the difference between depression and the dark night, with guidance
for assisting those who are experiencing both processes simultane-
ously.¹⁰ The dark night cannot simply be dismissed on psychological
or theological grounds.

One cannot read Scripture without encountering, again and again,
narratives of God's people being led into seasons of unknowing,
times of detachment, dryness, emptiness, a darkness in which God,
for a time, seems to have disappeared. In the biblical narrative as
well as the stories of many of the great saints and mystics, the night
was real. For the lives of many Christians today, the mystery of the
night is real, even if they lack the vocabulary to describe it. The *via
negativa* is an essential element of Christian spirituality. Along with
William Johnston, then, I propose that the church is indeed moving
into the night, where we find ourselves surrounded by the great cloud
of witnesses.¹¹

9. Denys Turner, *The Darkness of God: Negativity in Christian Mysticism* (Cambridge: Cambridge University Press, 1995), 227.

10. Gerald May, *Care of Mind, Care of Spirit* (San Francisco: HarperSanFrancisco, 1992).

11. William Johnston (*Arise My Love*) writes with special attention to Christian
ecumenism and interfaith dialogue, suggesting that Christianity of the twenty-first
century will increasingly be oriented toward Christian mysticism rather than doctrinal commitments. The dark night of the church will, in Johnston's view, prepare
the church for this kind of presence and fundamental orientation. While I agree with
Johnston about the impending night of the church and appreciate his ecumenism, I
am less optimistic about some of Johnston's conclusions.

Bibliography

Abraham, William J. *The Logic of Evangelism*. Grand Rapids: Eerdmans, 1989.

Adams, Carole J., and Marie M. Fortune, eds. *Violence against Women and Children: A Christian Theological Sourcebook*. New York: Continuum, 1995.

Adams, John H. "Big Losses Predicted in the PCUSA." *The Layman Online*. www.layman.org/layman/news/2006-news/big-losses-projected.htm (accessed February 13, 2006).

Allender, Dan B. *The Wounded Heart: Hope for Adult Victims of Childhood Sexual Abuse*. Colorado Springs: Navpress, 1990.

American Institute on Domestic Violence. "Domestic Violence in the Workplace Statistics." www.aidv-usa.com/Statistics.htm (accessed September 14, 2007).

Anderson, Allen. *An Introduction to Pentecostalism*. Cambridge: Cambridge University Press, 2004.

Andrews, William, ed. *Sisters in the Spirit: Three Black Women's Autobiographies of the Nineteenth Century*. Bloomington, IN: Indiana University Press, 1986.

Arias, Mortimer. *Announcing the Reign of God: Evangelization and the Subversive Memory of Jesus*. 1984. Reprint, Lima, OH: Academic Renewal Press, 2001.

Baker, David, and Elaine Heath. *More Light on the Path*. Grand Rapids: Baker Academic, 1999.

Baker-Fletcher, Karen. "Voice, Vision, and Spirit: Black Preaching Women in Nineteenth Century America." In *Sisters Struggling in the Spirit: A Women of Color Theological Anthology*, edited by Nantawan Boonprasat Lewis, 31–42. Louisville: Women's Ministries Program Area National Ministries Division, Presbyterian Church (USA), 1994.

Balthasar, Hans Urs von. *Credo*. Introduction by Medard Kehl, translated by David Kipp. New York: Crossroad, 1990.

———. *Dare We Hope That All Men Be Saved? With a Short Discourse on Hell*. San Francisco: Ignatius Press, 1988.

———. "Faith and the Expectation of an Imminent End." *Communio: International Catholic Review* 26 (Winter 1999): 687–97.

———. *My Work: In Retrospect*. San Francisco: Ignatius Press, 1993.

Baraka. DVD. Directed by Ron Fricke. Mpi Home Studio, 2001.

Barna Group. "Number of Unchurched Adults Has Nearly Doubled since 1991." *The Barna Update*, May 4, 2004. www.barna.org/FlexPage.aspx ?Page=BarnaUpdate&BarnaUpdateID=163 (accessed September 14, 2007).

Bernard of Clairvaux. "Four Degrees of Love." In *Invitation to Christian Spirituality*, edited by John R. Tyson, 149–53. New York: Oxford University Press, 1999.

Berry, Wendell. *Life Is a Miracle: An Essay against Modern Superstition*. Washington, DC: Counterpoint, 2000.

Beumer, Jurjen. *Henri Nouwen: A Restless Seeking for God*. Translated by David E. Schlaver and Nancy Forest-Flier. New York: Crossroad, 1997.

Birot, Antoine. "God in Christ, Reconciling the World to Himself: Redemption in Balthasar." *Communio: International Catholic Review* 24 (Summer 1997): 259–85.

Blommestijn, Hein, et al. *The Footprints of Love: John of the Cross as Guide in the Wilderness*. Translated by John Vriend. Louvain: Peeters, 2000.

Bonaventure. *The Soul's Journey into God, the Tree of Life, the Life of St. Francis*. Classics of Western Spirituality. Translated and with an introduction by Ewert Cousins. New York: Paulist Press, 1978.

———. *The Works of Bonaventure*, vol. 2, *The Breviloquium*. Translated by José de Vinck. Paterson, NJ: St. Anthony Guild Press, 1963.

Bougerol, Guy J. *Introduction to the Works of Bonaventure.* Paterson, NJ: St. Anthony Guild Press, 1964.

Bouteneff, Vera, ed. *Father Arseny: A Cloud of Witnesses.* Crestwood, NY: St. Vladimir's Seminary Press, 2001.

———. *Father Arseny 1893–1973: Priest, Prisoner, Spiritual Father.* Crestwood, NY: St. Vladimir's Seminary Press, 2004.

Bowman, Leonard J. "Cosmic Exemplarism of Bonaventure." *Journal of Religion* (April 1975): 181–98.

Brueggemann, Walter. *Biblical Perspectives on Evangelism.* Nashville: Abingdon, 1993.

———. *Cadences of Home: Preaching among Exiles.* Louisville: Westminster John Knox, 1997.

———. *Genesis.* Atlanta: John Knox, 1982.

Cannon, Katie Geneva. "The Wounds of Jesus: Justification of Goodness in the Face of Manifold Evil." In *A Troubling in My Soul: Womanist Perspectives on Evil and Suffering,* edited by Emilie M. Townes, 219–31. Maryknoll, NY: Orbis, 1993.

Catherine of Genoa. *Purgation and Purgatory: The Spiritual Dialogue.* Classics of Western Spirituality. Translation and notes by Serge Hughes. New York: Paulist Press, 1979.

Chambers, Oswald. *My Utmost for His Highest.* New York: Dodd, Mead & Co., 1935.

Chaves, Mark. *Congregations in America.* Cambridge: Harvard University Press, 2004.

Council on Biblical Manhood and Womanhood. "The Danvers Statement on Biblical Manhood and Womanhood." www.cbmw.org/Resources/Articles/The-Danvers-Statement (accessed March 20, 2008).

Cox, Harvey. *Fire from Heaven: The Rise of Pentecostal Spirituality and the Reshaping of Religion for the 21st Century.* Cambridge, MA: Da Capo Press, 2001.

Darragh, Neil. "Adjusting to the Newcomer: Theology and Ecotheology." *Pacifica* 13 (June 2000): 160–80.

Dart, John. "Stressed Out: Why Pastors Leave." *The Christian Century* 120, no. 24 (November 29, 2003): 8–9.

"Data Bite," *Christian Century* 120, no. 18 (September 6, 2003): 13.

Divorce Magazine. "U.S. Divorce Statistics." www.divorcemag.com/statistics/statsUS.shtml (accessed September 14, 2007).

Edwards, Denis. *Ecology at the Heart of Faith*. Maryknoll, NY: Orbis, 2006.

Egan, Harvey D. "Christian Apophatic and Kataphatic Mysticisms." *Theological Studies* 39 (September 1978): 399–426.

Ehrenreich, Barbara. *Nickel and Dimed: On (Not) Getting By in America*. New York: Metropolitan/Owl, 2001.

FaithTrust Institute. "Q&A." www.faithtrustinstitute.org (accessed September 14, 2007).

Finke, Roger, and Rodney Stark. *The Churching of America 1776–2005*. New Brunswick, NJ: Rutgers University Press, 2005.

Flora, Jerry R. "Searching for the Adequate Life: The Devotional Theology of Thomas R. Kelly." *Spirituality Today* 42, no. 1 (Spring, 1990). www.spiritualitytoday.org/spir2day/904214flora.html (accessed August 13, 2007).

Foote, Catherine J. *Survivor Prayers: Talking with God about Childhood Sexual Abuse*. Louisville: Westminster John Knox, 1994.

Foote, Julia. "A Brand Plucked from the Fire: An Autobiographical Sketch." In *Sisters in the Spirit: Three Black Women's Autobiographies of the Nineteenth Century*, edited and with an introduction by William Andrews, 161–234. Bloomington, IN: Indiana University Press, 1986.

Ford, Michael. *Wounded Prophet*. New York: Doubleday, 1999.

Fox, Matthew, ed. *Hildegard of Bingen's Book of Divine Works*. Santa Fe, NM: Bear, 1987.

French, R. M., trans. *The Way of a Pilgrim: And the Pilgrim Continues His Way*. San Francisco: HarperSanFrancisco, 1991.

General Council on Finance and Administration. The United Methodist Church. "2005 Preliminary Statistics Report Executive Summary." www.gcfa.org/PDFs/HPWN2005PreliminaryStatisticsReportExecSummary.pdf (accessed April 4, 2008).

Georg-Gadamer, Hans. *Truth and Method*. Rev. ed. New York: Continuum, 1991.

Gore, Al. *An Inconvenient Truth*. DVD. Produced by Lawrence Bender, Laurie David, and Scott Burns. Directed by Davis Guggenheim. Paramount, 2006.

Green, Linda. "United Methodist Attendance Rises, but Membership Continues Down." www.umc.org/site/c.gjJTJbMUIuE/b.880375/k.EA3C/United_Methodist_attendance_rises_but_membership_continues_down.htm (accessed September 14, 2007).

Groeschel, Benedict J. *Healing the Original Wound: Reflections on the Meaning of Salvation*. Cincinnati: Servant Publications, 1993.

Guder, Darrell, ed. *Missional Church*. Grand Rapids: Eerdmans, 1998.

Guyon, Jeanne Marie Bouvier de La Motte. *Experiencing the Depths of Jesus Christ*. Translated and edited by Gene Edwards. Augusta, ME: Christian Books Publishing House, 1975.

Hall, Thelma. *Too Deep for Words*. Mahwah, NJ: Paulist Press, 1988.

Harkness, Georgia. *The Dark Night of the Soul*. Nashville: Abingdon, 1945.

Harris, Sam. *The End of Faith: Religion, Terror and the Future of Reason*. New York: Norton, 2005.

Hassey, Janette. *No Time for Silence: Evangelical Women in Public Ministry around the Turn of the Century*. Grand Rapids: Academie, 1986.

Hayes, Zachary. "Incarnation and Creation in the Theology of St. Bonaventure." In *Studies Honoring Ignatius Charles Brady, Friar Minor*, edited by Romano Stephen Almagno and Conrad L. Harkins, 309–30. St. Bonaventure, NY: Franciscan Institute, 1976.

———. *Visions of a Future*. New Theology Studies 8. Edited by Peter C. Phan. Collegeville, MN: Liturgical Press, 1989.

Hildegard von Bingen. Quoted in *Vision: The Music of Hildegard von Bingen*. Hollywood, CA: Angel Records, 1994.

Hitchens, Christopher. *God Is Not Great: How Religion Poisons Everything*. New York: Twelve, 2007.

Houselander, Caryll. *The Reed of God*. 1976. Reprint, Allen, TX: Christian Classics, 1991.

Hügel, Friedrich von. *The Mystical Element of Religion*. 1923. Reprint, New York: Crossroad, 1999.

Hurnard, Hannah. *Hinds Feet on High Places*. Wheaton: Tyndale, 1986.

Ignatius of Loyola. *Spiritual Exercises and Selected Works*. Classics of Western Spirituality. Edited by George E. Ganss. Mahwah, NJ: Paulist Press, 1991.

———. "Surrender." In *The Living Testament: The Essential Writings of Christianity Since the Bible*, edited by M. Basil Pennington, Alan Jones, and Mark Booth, 224. San Francisco: Harper & Row, 1985.

Illusion Works, L.L.C. "Perceptual Ambiguity." http://psylux.psych.tu-dresden.de/i1/kaw/diverses%20Material/www.illusionworks.com/html/perceptual_ambiguity.html (accessed September 14, 2007).

Ingersoll, Julie. *Evangelical Christian Women: War Stories in the Gender Battles*. New York: New York University Press, 2003.

Institute for Plastination. "Body Worlds: An Anatomical Success Story." www .bodyworlds.com/en/prelude.html (accessed September 14, 2007).

Jenkins, Philip. *The Next Christendom*. New York: Oxford University Press, 2002.

John of the Cross. *Selected Writings*. Classics of Western Spirituality. Edited by Kieran Kavanaugh and Ernest E. Larkin. New York: Paulist Press, 1987.

Johnston, William. *Arise My Love: Mysticism for a New Era*. Maryknoll, NY: Orbis, 2000.

Jones, Scott. *The Evangelistic Love of God and Neighbor*. Nashville: Abingdon, 2003.

Jones, T. Canby. *Thomas R. Kelly As I Remember Him*. Wallingford, PA: Pendle Hill Publications, 1988.

Julian of Norwich. *Showings*. Classics of Western Spirituality. Edited by Edmund College and James Walsh. New York: Paulist Press, 1978.

Jung, Hee-Soo. "Hospitality in the Midst of Conflict: God's Grace and Our Practice." Lecture presented at the Spiritual Leaders Conference, Nashville, TN, July 31, 2007.

Kallenberg, Brad J. *Live to Tell: Evangelism in a Postmodern Age*. Grand Rapids: Brazos, 2002.

Keating, Thomas. *Open Mind, Open Heart: The Contemplative Dimension of the Gospel*. New York: Continuum, 1995.

Kelly, Thomas R. *A Testament of Devotion*. New York: Harper & Brothers, 1941.

Kirvan, John J. *Love without Measure: The Spirituality of Service of Mother Teresa*. Notre Dame, IN: Ave Maria Press, 2004.

Kluger, Jeffrey, et al. "Is God in Our Genes?" *Time*, October 25, 2004. www .time.com/time/magazine/article/0,9171,995465-3,00.html (accessed September 14, 2007).

LeClerc, Diane. *Holiness of Heart: Gender, Sin and Holiness in Historical Perspective*. Lanham, MD: Scarecrow, 2001.

Lerman, Kristina. "The Life and Works of Hildegard von Bingen (1098–1179)." www.fordham.edu/halsall/med/hildegarde.html (accessed September 14, 2007).

Lewis, Nantawan Boonprasat, ed. *Sisters Struggling in the Spirit: A Women of Color Theological Anthology*. Louisville: Women's Ministries Program Area National Ministries Division, Presbyterian Church (USA), n.d.

Lindbergh, Anne Morrow. *Gift from the Sea*. New York: Vintage, 1978.

Linn, Dennis, Sheila Fabricant Linn, Matthew Linn, and Francisco Miranda. *Good Goats: Healing Our Images of God*. New York: Paulist Press, 1993.

Llewelyn, Robert. *All Shall Be Well*. New York: Paulist Press, 1982.

Martin, David. *Tongues of Fire: The Explosion of Pentecostalism in Latin America*. Oxford: Blackwell, 1993.

May, Gerald. *Care of Mind, Care of Spirit*. San Francisco: HarperSanFrancisco, 1992.

———. *The Dark Night of the Soul: A Psychiatrist Explores the Connection between Darkness and Spiritual Growth*. San Francisco: HarperSanFrancisco, 2004.

McBrien, Richard P., ed. *The Harper Collins Encyclopedia of Catholicism*. San Francisco: HarperSanFrancisco, 1995.

McGinn, Bernard. *The Presence of God*. Vol. 1, *The Foundations of Mysticism*. New York: Crossroad, 1992.

McGonigle, Thomas D. "Three Ways." In *The New Dictionary of Catholic Spirituality*, edited by Michael Downey, 963–65. Collegeville, MN: Liturgical Press, 1993.

McIntosh, Mark A. "Christology." In *The Cambridge Companion to Hans Urs von Balthasar*, edited by Edward T. Oakes and David Moss, 26–27. Cambridge: Cambridge University Press, 2004.

———. *Mystical Theology*. Malden, MA: Blackwell, 1998.

McLaren, Brian. *A Generous Orthodoxy: Why I Am a Missional, Evangelical, Post/Protestant, Liberal/Conservative, Mystical/Poetic, Biblical, Charismatic/Contemplative, Fundamentalist/Calvinist, Anabaptist/Anglican, Methodist, Catholic, Green, Incarnational, Depressed-Yet-Hopeful, Emergent, Unfinished Christian*. Grand Rapids: Zondervan, 2004.

———. *More Ready Than You Realize: Evangelism as Dance in the Postmodern Matrix*. Grand Rapids: Zondervan, 2002.

Mechthild of Magdeburg. *The Flowing Light of the Godhead*. Classics of Western Spirituality. Translated and with an introduction by Frank Tobin. Preface by Margot Schmidt. New York: Paulist Press, 1998.

"Methodists See More No-Growth Churches." *Christian Century* 123, no. 8 (April 18, 2006): 16.

Miller, Susan. *Women in Mark's Gospel.* New York: T&T Clark International, 2004.

Monti, Dominic. "St. Bonaventure." In *The Harper Collins Encyclopedia of Catholicism*, edited by Richard P. McBrien, 189–90. San Francisco: HarperSanFrancisco, 1995.

Morse, David. *Testimony: John Woolman on Today's Global Economy.* Wallingford, PA: Pendle Hill Publications, 2001.

Mother Teresa. *In My Own Words.* Compiled by José Luis Gonázles-Balado. New York: Gramercy, 1997.

Mother Teresa and Brian Kolodiejchuk. *Come Be My Light.* New York: Doubleday, 2007.

Moulton, Phillips P. Introduction to *The Journal and Major Essays of John Woolman*, by John Woolman, edited by Phillips P. Moulton, 3–16. Richmond, IN: Friends United Press, 1989.

Murk-Jansen, Saskia. *Brides in the Desert: The Spirituality of the Beguines.* Maryknoll, NY: Orbis, 1998.

Muto, Susan. *John of the Cross for Today: The Dark Night.* Notre Dame, IN: Ave Maria Press, 1994.

National Center for Victims of Crime. "Child Sexual Abuse." www.ncvc .org/ncvc/main.aspx?dbName=DocumentViewer&DocumentID=32315 (accessed September 14, 2007).

National Coalition against Domestic Violence. "Domestic Violence Facts." www.ncadv.org/files/domesticviolencefacts.pdf (accessed September 14, 2007).

National Council of Churches. "2006 Yearbook of Churches Reflects Robust Immigrant History in US." *News from the National Council of Churches.* www.ncccusa.org/news/060330yearbook1.html (accessed September 14, 2007).

———. "Benevolences Up, Membership Stable: 2001 Yearbook Reports." *News from the National Council of Churches.* www.ncccusa.org/news/ 01news15.html (accessed September 14, 2007).

Nemeck, Francis Kelly, and Marie Theresa Coombs. *O Blessed Night.* New York: Alba House, 1991.

Newbigin, Lesslie. *The Open Secret.* Rev. ed. Grand Rapids: Eerdmans, 1995.

Newsom, Carol A., and Sharon H. Ringe, eds. *The Women's Bible Commentary*. Louisville: Westminster John Knox, 1998.

Niditch, Susan. "Genesis." In *The Women's Bible Commentary*, edited by Carol A. Newsom and Sharon H. Ringe, 13–29. Louisville: Westminster John Knox, 1998.

Nouwen, Henri J. M. *The Inner Voice of Love: The Journey through Anguish to Freedom*. New York: Doubleday, 1996.

———. *In the Name of Jesus: Reflections on Christian Leadership*. New York: Crossroad, 1992.

———. *Life of the Beloved*. New York: Crossroad, 1992.

———. *The Return of the Prodigal Son*. New York: Image, 1994.

———. *Sabbatical Journey: The Diary of His Final Year*. New York: Crossroad, 1998.

———. *Spiritual Journals*. New York: Continuum, 1999.

———. *A Tribute to Henri Nouwen: The "Cross Currents" Interviews*. Vision TV, 1994.

Oakes, Edward T., and David Moss, eds. *The Cambridge Companion to Hans Urs von Balthasar*. Cambridge: Cambridge University Press, 2004.

Oden, Thomas C., ed. *Phoebe Palmer*. Sources of American Spirituality. New York: Paulist Press, 1988.

O'Laughlin, Michael. *God's Beloved: A Spiritual Biography of Henri Nouwen*. Maryknoll, NY: Orbis, 2004.

Olsen, Ted, and Todd Hertz. "How the Clergy Sexual Abuse Scandal Affects Evangelical Churches." *Christianity Today*, March 20, 2002. www .christianitytoday.com/ct/2002/110/31.0.html (accessed April 2006).

OMB Watch. "IRS Audits Church for Anti-War Sermon." www.ombwatch .org/article/articleview/3167/1/403 (accessed September 14, 2007).

Outward Bound. "About Outward Bound." www.outwardbound.org (accessed September 14, 2007).

Palmer, Phoebe. *Faith and Its Effects: Or Fragments from My Portfolio*. 1854. Reprint, Salem, OH: Schmul Publishing Co., 1999.

———. *Incidental Illustrations of the Economy of Salvation, Its Doctrines and Duties*. Boston: Henry V. Degen, 1855. Selections republished as *Full Salvation: Its Doctrine and Duties*. Salem, OH: Schmul Publishing Co., n.d.

———. *Promise of the Father*. 1859. Reprint, Salem, OH: Schmul Publishing Co., n.d.

―――. *The Way of Holiness*. 1843. Reprint, Salem, OH: Schmul Publishing Co., 1988.

Park, Andrew Sung. *The Wounded Heart of God*. Nashville: Abingdon, 1993.

Park, Andrew Sung, and Susan L. Nelson, eds. *The Other Side of Sin*. Albany: State University of New York Press, 2001.

Pennington, M. Basil. *True Self, False Self*. New York: Crossroad, 2000.

Penn-Lewis, Jessie. *Fruitful Living*. Dorset, UK: Overcomer Literature Trust, n.d.

Pohl, Christine, and Nicola Hoggard Creegan. *Living on the Boundaries: Evangelical Women, Feminism and the Theological Academy*. Downers Grove, IL: InterVarsity, 2006.

Pope-Levison, Priscilla. *Turn the Pulpit Loose: Two Centuries of American Women Evangelists*. New York: Palgrave MacMillan, 2004.

"Presbyterian Losses Largest Since '83." *Christian Century* 121, no. 13 (June 29, 2004): 13.

Pui-lan, Kwok. *Postcolonial Imagination and Feminist Theology*. Louisville: Westminster John Knox, 2005.

Rainforest Foundation. "The Destruction of Rainforests." www.rainforest foundationuk.org/s-The%20Destruction%20of%20Rainforests (accessed July 20, 2007).

Rape Victim Advocacy Program. "Myths and Facts—Child Sexual Abuse." www.rvap.org/pages/myths_and_facts_about_child_sexual_abuse (accessed September 14, 2007).

Raser, Harold E. *Phoebe Palmer: Her Life and Thought*. Lewiston, NY: Edwin Mellen, 1987.

Reuters. "Are You a Giver? Brain Scan Tells the Truth." www.msnbc.msn .com/id/16740765 (accessed January 21, 2007).

Richard Dawkins Foundation for Reason and Science. http://richarddawkins .net/foundation (accessed September 14, 2007).

Rivers, Dan. "Without a Home: Refugees in Crisis." *Anderson Cooper 360*. http://transcripts.cnn.com/TRANSCRIPTS/0706/20/acd.02.html (accessed June 20, 2007).

Roberts, Tyler. "Between the Lines: Exceeding Historicism in the Study of Religion." *Journal of the American Academy of Religion* 74, no. 3 (September 2006): 697–719.

Rohr, Richard. *Everything Belongs*. Rev. ed. New York: Crossroad, 2003.

Ruether, Rosemary Radford. *Visionary Women: Three Medieval Mystics.* Minneapolis: Augsburg Fortress, 2002.

Sahadat, John. "The Interreligious Study of Mysticism and a Sense of Universality." *Journal of Ecumenical Studies* (Spring 1985): 292–311.

Savage, Anne, and Nicholas Watson, trans. and eds. *"Ancrene Wisse" and Associated Works.* Classics of Western Spirituality. New York: Paulist Press, 1991.

Schlosser, Eric. *Fast Food Nation.* New York: Houghton Mifflin, 2001.

Scott, David. *A Revolution of Love: The Meaning of Mother Teresa.* Chicago: Loyola Press, 2005.

Scruton, Roger. *Sexual Desire: A Moral Philosophy of the Erotic.* New York: Continuum, 1986.

Simons, Walter. *Cities of Ladies: Beguine Communities in the Medieval Low Countries, 1200–1565.* Philadelphia: University of Pennsylvania Press, 2001.

Sleeth, Matthew. "The Future of Eco-Evangelism." *AlterNet*, April 23, 2005. www.alternet.org/environment/21847?page=2 (accessed April 12, 2007).

Smith, Andy. "Christian Conquest and the Sexual Colonization of Native Women." In *Violence against Women and Children: A Christian Theological Sourcebook*, edited by Carole J. Adams and Marie M. Fortune, 377–403. New York: Continuum, 1995.

"Southern Baptists Decline in Baptisms, Make Evangelism a First Priority." *The Christian Post* (April 20, 2006). www.christianpost.com/article/church/2605/section/southern.baptists.decline.in.baptisms.make.evangelism.first.priority/1.htm.

Steere, Douglas V. "A Biographic Memoir." In *A Testament of Devotion*, by Thomas R. Kelly, 1–28. New York: Harper & Brothers, 1941.

Stenger, Victor J. *God: The Failed Hypothesis, How Science Shows That God Does Not Exist.* Amherst, NY: Prometheus, 2007.

Sting. "If You Love Somebody, Set Them Free." *The Very Best of Sting and the Police.* A&M, 2002.

Strom, Kay Marshall, and Michele Rickett. *Daughters of Hope: Stories of Witness and Courage in the Face of Persecution.* Downers Grove, IL: InterVarsity, 2003.

Sweet, Leonard, ed. *The Church in Emerging Culture: Five Perspectives.* Grand Rapids: Zondervan, 2003.

Taves, Ann. *Fits, Trances and Visions: Experiencing Religion and Explaining Experience from Wesley to James*. Princeton, NJ: Princeton University Press, 1999.

Thompson, Andrew C. "Decline in Young Leadership Threatens Methodism's Future." *United Methodist Reporter* 152, no. 52 (May 5, 2006): 7B.

Thompson, William M. *Christology and Spirituality*. New York: Crossroad, 1991.

———. *Fire and Light: The Saints and Theology*. New York: Paulist Press, 1987.

Thurman, Howard. "Mysticism and the Experience of Love." In *For the Inward Journey: The Writings of Howard Thurman*, edited by Anne Spencer Thurman with an introduction by Vincent Harding, 189–95. New York: Harcourt, Brace, and Jovanovich, 1984.

Tierra Nueva. "The People's Seminary." www.peoplesseminary.org/The PeoplesSeminary.html (accessed September 14, 2007).

Tolles, Frederick B. Introduction to *The Journal of John Woolman and a Plea for the Poor*, by John Woolman, edited by Frederick B. Tolles, v–xii. New York: Corinth Books, 1961.

Tolson, Jay. "Is There Room for the Soul?" *U.S. News & World Report*, October 15, 2006. http://health.usnews.com/usnews/health/articles/061015/23soul .htm (accessed September 14, 2007).

Townes, Emilie M., ed. *A Troubling in My Soul: Womanist Perspectives on Evil and Suffering*. Maryknoll, NY: Orbis, 1993.

Trible, Phyllis. *Texts of Terror: Literary-Feminist Readings of Biblical Narratives*. London: SCM, 2002.

Tucker, Ruth, and Walter Liefeld. *Daughters of the Church: Women and Ministry from the New Testament Times to the Present*. Grand Rapids: Academie, 1987.

Turner, Denys. *The Darkness of God: Negativity in Christian Mysticism*. Cambridge: Cambridge University Press, 1995.

Underhill, Evelyn. *Mysticism*. New York: Meridian, 1955.

———. *Practical Mysticism*. Columbus, OH: Ariel, 1986.

UNICEF. "Facts on Children." www.unicef.org/media/media_9475.html (accessed July 5, 2007).

Volf, Miroslav. *Exclusion and Embrace: A Theological Exploration of Identity, Otherness, and Reconciliation*. Nashville: Abingdon, 1996.

Wacker, Grant. *Heaven Below: Early Pentecostals and American Culture.* Cambridge: Harvard University Press, 2001.

Wainwright, Geoffrey. "Eschatology." In *The Cambridge Companion to Hans Urs von Balthasar*, edited by Edward T. Oakes and David Moss, 113. Cambridge: Cambridge University Press, 2004.

Wallace, Mark I. *The Second Naiveté: Barth, Ricoeur, and the New Yale Theology.* 2nd ed. Macon, GA: Mercer University Press, 1995.

Ware, Kallistos. *The Inner Kingdom.* Crestwood, NY: St. Vladimir's Seminary Press, 2001.

Watson, Nicholas, and Jacqueline Jenkins, eds. *The Writings of Julian of Norwich.* University Park, PA: Pennsylvania State University Press, 2006.

Weems, Lovett H., Jr. "Leadership for Reaching Emerging Generations." *Circuit Rider* (March–April 2006): 4–7.

Westermann, Claus. *Genesis 1–11.* Minneapolis: Augsburg, 1984.

Wheatley, Richard, ed. *The Life and Letters of Mrs. Phoebe Palmer.* 1881. Reprint, New York: Garland Publishing, 1984.

White, Charles Edward. *The Beauty of Holiness: Phoebe Palmer as Theologian, Revivalist, Feminist and Humanitarian.* Grand Rapids: Zondervan, 1986.

Wilken, Robert L. *Remembering the Christian Past.* Grand Rapids: Eerdmans, 1995.

Witherington, Ben, III. *The Gospel of Mark: A Socio-Rhetorical Commentary.* Grand Rapids: Eerdmans, 2001.

Wood, David J. "The Conditions of Call." *Congregations* (March–April 2001). www.alban.org/ShowArticle.asp?ID=114 (accessed September 14, 2007).

Woolman, John. *The Journal and Major Essays of John Woolman.* Edited by Phillips P. Moulton. Richmond, IN: Friends United Press, 1989.

_____. *The Journal of John Woolman and a Plea for the Poor.* Edited by Frederick B. Tolles. New York: Corinth Books, 1961.

Wuthnow, Robert. *The Crisis in the Churches.* New York: Oxford University Press, 1997.

Yong, Amos. *The Spirit Poured Out on All Flesh: Pentecostalism and the Possibility of Global Spirituality.* Grand Rapids: Baker Academic, 2005.

Yuen, Wai Man. *Religious Experience and Interpretation: Memory as the Path to the Knowledge of God in Julian of Norwich's Showings.* New York: Peter Lang, 2003.

Index